"With scholarly wisdom and inspirational devotion Malcolm invites us to encounter the real Jesus. Undoubtedly 40 unmissable days, each one holding the potential to change our lives. Superb!"

– **Catherine Campbell**, author of *God Knows Your Name*

"Malcolm's simple reflections on the various facets of Jesus' character reflect his own commitment to Christ – uncluttered, uncompromising, accessible and passionate. Digesting these daily devotionals will draw you deeper and closer to God's heart."

– **Simon Guillebaud**, author of *Choose Life*

Within each entry of this short, easy to read, collection of devotionals, Malcolm takes the reader on the great journey of experiencing Jesus. This straightforward and vast look at the life of Christ will deepen your understanding of Him and propel you out to live the Jesus way of life. 40 Days With Jesus *is a life-giving read!*

– **Rob Peabody**, author of *Citizen*

Also by Malcolm Duncan:

Kingdom Come

Risk Takers

Unbelievable

40 Days with Jesus

An invitation to know him better

Malcolm Duncan

MONARCH
BOOKS

Oxford UK, and Grand Rapids, USA

Published by Monarch Books
an imprint of Lion Hudson plc
Wilkinson House, Jordan Hill Road,
Oxford OX2 8DR, England
Email: monarch@lionhudson.com
www.lionhudson.com/monarch

ISBN 978 0 85721 644 1
e-ISBN 978 0 85721 645 8

First edition 2015

A catalogue record for this book is available from the British Library

Printed and bound in the UK, January 2015, LH26

This book is dedicated to a number of people:

The late Maureen and Gilbert Hill – my great-aunt and great-uncle. They played a significant role in my conversion and I saw Jesus beautifully revealed in their lives.

Lyndon and Celia Bowring, in whom I see Jesus so very clearly.

Brenda and Lionel Sloggett, whose lives have reflected Christ to me so very often.

Those with whom I have walked the path of sorrow and loss – you have shown me so much of Christ.

My wife, Debbie, and four children, Matthew, Benjamin, Anna, and Riodhna. I see Jesus in you every day – thank you all.

Lastly, and most importantly, thank you, Lord Jesus, for your love, your grace, and your mercy.

Contents

Acknowledgments

Saying thank you at the beginning of a book should never be just a formality; rather it is a joy and a privilege.

Thank you, once again, to Tony Collins, Jenny Ward and all at the Lion Hudson/Monarch family. I am blessed to minister with you.

Thank you to all in the Gold Hill family who continually support and pray for me. It is an honour to walk with you and I am blessed beyond words. I am particularly grateful to my fellow elders, church council members and staff for their ongoing support and encouragement.

I want to offer a special word of thanks to my personal assistant, Maria Bond, without whom my job would be a great deal harder.

There is a great mood sweeping the church to make Jesus fit into our culture and our world. In our attempts to make him more palatable, I am convinced we are denuding his life and message of its power and beauty. While the words contained here are simple and straightforward, my prayer is that this little book will present the ministry and life of Jesus in a way that is true to the story of Scripture. It is written with the desire that those who are new to the faith or exploring it for the first time will meet the Jesus who changes lives and transforms destinies.

For those who already know and love Christ, it is my prayer that these words will deepen your love for him, remind you of his inestimable love for you and cause you to explore his life and its message with even greater passion and purpose.

The good things about this book are the results of the input of many people. The mistakes and shortcomings are mine and mine alone.

Introduction

This little book is a humble and flawed attempt to introduce you to some of the aspects of the character and the life of Jesus Christ. If someone else were writing it, they would no doubt use different verses and different passages. In fact, if I were writing it again, I could easily use a hundred different verses and passages. I could write a little book like this every year for the rest of my life and use a hundred different passages every single time. There's a simple reason for that (as I pick up in my first reflection): there is just no way to capture the wonder and the beauty of Jesus.

What I have given you are reflections on Jesus. I haven't set out to write a thorough systematic theology or a blow-by-blow account of who Jesus was. Instead, I have tried to keep my thoughts and reflections simple, straightforward, and devotional in nature. My aim is neither to fill your head with more and more ideas nor to cram as much theological truth into the short space you may have to read one of these reflections. Rather, I want to try to warm your heart towards Jesus. My prayer is that the Holy Spirit, the Third Person of the Trinity in whom we Christians believe, will draw you into a few moments of reflection on the life and the truth of Jesus Christ. Not only do I pray you will begin to read about Jesus; I also pray you will talk to him.

40 Days with Jesus is actually sixty-four small passages about Jesus made up of a total of 139 verses. There are many ways in which I could have divided the material, but I have chosen to do three things.

Firstly, I have taken some of the important truths about who Jesus is and what he has done and set them out in forty reflections. My hope is that as you read them, you'll discover for the first time – or you'll remember – just how central Jesus is to Christianity. I know it goes without saying, but you would be surprised how many people have forgotten that to be a Christian is to be a follower of Jesus Christ. Jesus didn't come to establish a religion; he came to change lives and to deal with the barriers that exist between God and us. He came to save the world. Unfortunately, we Christians are very good at boxing him in. He doesn't like boxes – they feel a little too much like tombs, and Jesus has a tendency to refuse to stay in those…

Secondly, I have written a short prayer that accompanies each reflection. I hope it will help you to go beyond the rush of reading a section too quickly. If the little prayer helps you to talk to God more deeply on your own, that is great. If it is the only prayer you use for the day you read the reflection, that's great too. Please do read these slowly and thoughtfully if you can. My reflections are illustrative, not exhaustive. I intend them to be an invitation to intimacy rather than a final word. You might not yet be a Christian. If not, I hope you meet the Jesus I have met – he is a wonderful friend! You might be a Christian already. If so, I hope your relationship with Jesus deepens. You might be reading *40 Days with Jesus* on your own – if so, I hope it is a special time for you. You might be reading it as part of a small group or a church – if you are, I hope it sparks some wonderful discussions and perhaps even some worship.

Thirdly, because I firmly believe that Jesus can be found throughout the Bible, I am working on a volume to accompany *40 Days with Jesus* called *Jesus – Book by Book* which will take just one passage from each of the sixty-six books of the Bible and unpack something of the character and heart of Jesus that can be found in the book. Such an exercise could go in a hundred different directions for each book of the Bible, but I have had great fun choosing the themes for that volume. I hope you like them when it is finally published.

Whoever you are, however you are reading this little book, and whatever your reasons for doing so, may you meet Jesus in a way that will change your life forever.

Sola Deo Gloria.

Malcolm Duncan (Buckinghamshire, June 2014)

A Word About Language

Throughout the text of *40 Days with Jesus* you will notice that I have spelled the name "Satan" with a small "s". This is intentional. It is not to convey that he is not a real person, but rather that his name is actually a transliteration of a word that means "accuser". I choose not to give him the satisfaction of a capital "S".

DAY 1

Beautiful Beyond Words

But there are also many other things that Jesus did; if every one of them were written down, I suppose that the world itself could not contain the books that would be written.

John 21:25

How do you fit the ocean into a thimble? How can you capture the beauty of the one you love in a snapshot? How do you explain the inexplicable?

Well, it is impossible.

Jesus Christ is quite simply the most beautiful, caring, and loving person you could ever meet. He is also the most breathtakingly honest friend you could ever have. Spend any time with him at all and you will recognize that his love disarms you. He leaves you realizing just how selfish, spiteful, and silly you can be, but he also leaves you with the most incredible gift – the gift of his love. Love that will undo you and then remake you. Love that will break you and then remodel you.

I have known him as my friend since 1986, and he has never let me down. I have failed him many times. I have hurt him, lied to him, run away from him, and insulted him. When I think of the times I have been embarrassed by him or been afraid to tell other people about him, I blush. Yet what leaves me speechless is that he has never been embarrassed by me. He has never been afraid to defend me. He has never walked away from me. He just won't let me go. There aren't enough words in the universe to explain what he is like. I am not the first person to feel that way, and I certainly will not be the last.

One of Jesus' disciples was a man called John. John intrigues me. His name is attributed to five books in the Bible. Firstly, the Gospel of John, then three general epistles towards the end of the New Testament, and finally the very last book of the Bible – the book of Revelation. John was the only one of the twelve apostles to die a natural death. The story goes that he settled down in Ephesus (in modern-day Turkey) and lived out his years there. Some suggest that he would often be carried on a stretcher to the gatherings of his fellow Christians and they would ask him to tell them stories about Jesus.

John certainly had a way with words. His images of light, life, hope, joy, and purpose dance from the pages of the New Testament like the notes of a symphony. You can hear the depth of his relationship with Jesus through his language. He gives us pictures of Jesus turning water into wine, healing an official's son, healing a man who could not walk, feeding thousands, walking on water, giving sight to the blind, and raising the dead. Each time he tells us such a story, he shows us something about Jesus. Jesus brings a new kingdom of joy and purpose, he has overcome sickness and fear, he shows us the right path to walk, he is the bread and wine of our lives, he is sovereign over creation, he restores our spiritual sight, and he brings us back to life.

Yet John knows that all the books in the world could not explain the kindness and the power and the holiness and the specialness of Jesus. Jesus is more than a point of study or explanation for John. Jesus is John's friend. Jesus is John's Saviour. Jesus has brought God to John. It is little wonder John cannot explain Jesus to us.

I can't either, but I hope – no, I *pray* that you will read these words and that you will discover that, however beautiful you think Jesus is, he is actually far more beautiful than that. However much you think you know him, I pray that you will realize just how much *more* there is to know of him. Perhaps most of all, I pray that you will not simply "study" Jesus as you read these words; I pray that you will meet him and that he will do something in your heart so that you will never, ever be the same again.

He really is beautiful beyond words.

Prayer

Lord,
Help me to see you with new eyes.
Let me encounter you as I read these pages.
Whisper my name.
Challenge my assumptions.
Break my preconceptions.
Help me to meet you in a fresh, new, and living way.
Move me beyond the familiar and into the unknown.

Undo me with your love.
Challenge me with your holiness.
Transform me with your power.
Draw me with your beauty.
Breathe upon me by your Spirit.
Amen.

DAY 2

God's Plan A

But God knew what would happen, and his prearranged plan was carried out when Jesus was betrayed. With the help of lawless Gentiles, you nailed him to a cross and killed him. But God released him from the horrors of death and raised him back to life, for death could not keep him in its grip.

Acts 2:23–24 (NLT)

I've been involved in several "rescue" operations in my time! Sorting out terrible mistakes I have made or fixing mistakes that someone else has made becomes an occupational hazard when you are a pastor. Come to think of it, that is also true when you are a son, or a father or a husband, or a friend! Life has a way of coming "unstuck".

If we are not careful, we can end up thinking that the life and ministry of Jesus Christ on the earth was a little bit like that – a rescue operation for a plan that went wrong. Somehow, we can think that God needed to come up with an emergency plan to rescue a world that was, well, frankly, spinning out of control. And the world certainly is spinning out of control. Whether it is politics, economics, or the environment, we are not in a great place. Something needs to change…

It would be a mistake, however, to approach the life and the ministry of Jesus with the view that it was some kind of Plan B. At the heart of Christian belief is the conviction that God deliberately and intentionally sent his Son, Jesus, to redeem a fallen world and to rescue a deeply broken creation. Instead, before the process of creation itself began, God knew that in sharing life with us (and that is, in effect, what creation does), and in giving us the freedom to reject him, the only way the world could be restored, and the only way we could be rescued from our own selfish decisions and attitudes, would be if he were to directly involve himself in the process of both creation and redemption.

There are many ways in which Christians look at the question of how God made the world. Some believe in a literal seven-day event. Others believe in an evolutionary process that took place over billions of years. Still others believe in "epochs" or "periods" of creation when different things happened and developed. What all Christians share in their view of the world is that God is the Creator. Everything that is good that has been created finds its source in God – we see that in the whole creation story in Genesis 1 with the repeated phrase, "it was good".

When humanity emerges in the first pages of the Bible we read that God made us "in his image" and that he saw us as "very good". Yet in creating us, God also gave us choices and freedoms, otherwise we would be little more than robots or toys for him to play with. One of the fundamental choices he has given us is the ability to reject him and his instructions and to do things our way.

Even though these choices can result in great harm to ourselves or to others, God releases us from some kind of fatalistic grip and allows us to make up our own minds.

In the opening pages of the book of Genesis, we read of our ancestors' decisions to ignore God, and of the consequences of those decisions. Living according to our own plans and not God's is known in the Bible as "sin", and some of the consequences of sin are separation from God, suspicion and hostility towards one another, death, suffering, and pain. Sin also leaves us powerless to rescue ourselves, because even if we could do so, we would simply make the same mistakes again.

To rescue us, God must find a way of entering time and history in a tangible and visible way to deal with the fundamental brokenness in our lives and in our world – the consequences of our sin. We cannot "fix" the problem ourselves, so God must fix it for us. To fix the problem, he must find a way of addressing the brokenness which we have caused without removing the freedom of choice that he has given. God must come to us in person. He must come to us as God, yet he must also come to us as a human being just like us. The God who exists beyond time and history must enter history. He must carry the consequences of our sin for us to enable us to choose him. That is why he sends his Son, Jesus. The Son of God is both fully God and fully human. God knew, before he embarked on creation itself, that would be the cost of creating us – but he was willing to pay that price because he loved us even before he created us. In creating us, he knew he would also have to redeem us, and to redeem us, he knew it would cost him his Son.

Prayer

Lord,

I don't understand why you love me enough to rescue me.

Sometimes I don't even love myself that much.

As I look at my life, I see the times when I have really messed up and nobody has wanted to help.

So when I try to think of your willingness to enter history to rescue me, it leaves me puzzled.

I'm even more astounded that you would have willingly and gladly chosen to create the world and me in the first place, when you knew it would be inevitable that we would reject you and your rule over us.

Help me to see that your plan of redemption was chosen because of love.

Help me to discover the depth of your love and grace for me and for all who will call upon the name of your Son, Jesus.

Help me not only to read about Jesus, but also to meet him, to discover who he really is.

Amaze me with your grace.

Reveal yourself to me in a new way.

Help me understand how much it cost you to provide a way of redemption for me.

Amen.

DAY 3

Jesus Reflects God to Us

Long ago God spoke many times and in many ways to our ancestors through the prophets. And now in these final days, he has spoken to us through his Son. God promised everything to the Son as an inheritance, and through the Son he created the universe. The Son radiates God's own glory and expresses the very character of God, and he sustains everything by the mighty power of his command. When he had cleansed us from our sins, he sat down in the place of honour at the right hand of the majestic God in heaven. This shows that the Son is far greater than the angels, just as the name God gave him is greater than their names.

Hebrews 1:1–4 (NLT)

We do not need to guess what God is really like. Jesus Christ perfectly reflects God to us. He is like a perfect mirror, with no cracks or spots or blemishes. In him we see God's grace and beauty and kindness as well as God's holiness and power and majesty.

The writer of the book of Hebrews wants the recipients of his letter to understand that God has come to them *in Jesus* and that they need never be in any doubt again about what God is really like. Jesus is *better* than anything they have ever seen or heard before. He is the *complete* and *full* revelation of God to them. In a series of remarkable statements, the writer of Hebrews make this point over and over again – Jesus is better. Jesus is better than angels; he is better than Moses; he is better than the Law; he is better than the sabbath; he is better than the old priesthood; he is a better sacrifice; his is a better covenant.

The original recipients of this letter would have been as speechless as we are at reading such a powerful explanation of who Jesus was and is. How could it be possible that Jesus was *better?* The answer to that question lies in the opening words of the epistle to the Hebrews.

Jesus is not *just* a reflection of God; he is God himself, come to us in flesh. The Hebrew Bible is made up of the wonderful ways in which God spoke to his people, Israel. The prophets brought God's Word to God's people. They were the mouthpieces through whom God spoke. The words they brought were fully inspired and fully human. They were God's words spoken through God's servants. The prophets themselves were *conduits* through whom the Holy Spirit spoke God's words. Therefore their words were *both* fully inspired and fully human because they displayed the human personalities, culture, and language of the people speaking.

In Jesus, God is fully present and speaking. Jesus is not only a *conduit* of God to us because Jesus is God himself come to us. He not only *brings* God's word; he *is* God's Word. This is an astounding claim. Jesus is not just a messenger; he is the message as well.

If Jesus is the Word itself, doesn't that mean he was present and active in creation? That would put him on a place of equality with God. Could that be possible? That is exactly what the writer to the Hebrews argues in the opening lines of his letter.

The writer uses several powerful images to drive this incredible idea home. Jesus is the Son of God himself. That Son is both the One who inherits the universe and the One who is present and active in its creation!

Not only that, the Son shows us exactly, in every detail and in every way, what God is like. There is no flaw in the Son's representation of God to us. He *radiates* the very glory and majesty and power of God to those who see him. He does so continually, consistently, and clearly.

The Son – Jesus – is not only the central agent of creation; he is the continual sustainer of that creation. It is *still* his powerful Word that upholds the universe and all that is created.

The writer of the letter to the Hebrews uses a particularly powerful image to help us understand the extent of this perfect representation (see also Ephesians 1:3). The king would seal legal documents when he pressed his signet ring or his stamp into the wax poured upon the document. This "seal" would be a perfect representation of the king's power and authority and promise and would ensure that the document was fully and finally binding. Jesus is this "seal" to us!

We need never again wonder what God is like because he is perfectly seen in Jesus. If we want to know what God is really like, all we need do is look at the life, the attitude, the words, and the character of Jesus and what he has done for us!

Guesswork is not required – God has shown us his heart in the Lord Jesus Christ.

Prayer

Lord,

I can so very often forget what you are like.

I look around me and I see the suffering in the world and I wonder if you care.

I can see the struggles of those I love, or I experience struggles myself, and I quickly forget what you are like.

I can look at people in your church and think that because of their mistakes you must be flawed. I hear people describe you as a vengeful and angry God, and if I am not careful, I believe them and not your Word.

Remind me that I see you perfectly and beautifully reflected in your Son, the Lord Jesus. Help me to become so familiar with him that I will love you more deeply and revere you.

Thank you that the way you reveal yourself in the Hebrew Bible points forward to the complete and full revelation of who you are in your Son, the Lord Jesus. Thank you that there is no dichotomy between how you revealed yourself to Israel and how you reveal yourself through him.

Forgive me when I try to make you into nothing more than a talisman that approves of my every choice and never challenges me. Forgive me when I turn you into a tyrant who only ever disapproves of humanity.

Thank you that neither of these caricatures is true.

Thank you that I see your gentleness in the Lord Jesus, in the way he treated the failing, the forsaken, and the forgotten. Thank you that I see your forgiveness and grace in him.

Thank you that I see your holiness and your power in the Lord Jesus, in the way he challenged the self-righteous, in the way he spoke of the final judgment, in the way in which he defeated the evil one. Thank you that I see your majesty in him.

Help me not to sanitize Jesus or domesticate him. Help me not to sanitize you or domesticate you. Help me to worship you in your majesty, to praise you in your power, and to draw near to you in your tenderness and mercy.

Please change my wrong perceptions of you as I think about and engage with your Son, the Lord Jesus. Show me what you are like in new and fresh ways. Challenge my assumptions. Change my preconceptions.

Let me discover you with fresh and new excitement and let me continually learn new things about who you are and about your beauty and majesty. Deepen my experience of your love and holiness and make me more like you day by day.

Help me to reflect you to those around me in everything I am and in everything I do.

Amen.

DAY 4

Jesus, Son of Mary

And she gave birth to her firstborn son and wrapped him in swaddling cloths and laid him in a manger, because there was no place for them in the inn.

Luke 2:7 (ESV)

In the first few hundred years of the church's history, there was pretty much a continual battle about whether Jesus Christ was human or divine. Was he half human and half divine? Was he more human than divine? Was he more divine than human? Why did it matter? The great councils of the early church debated this issue again and again and again. Slowly, over several centuries and many decades, the answer emerged upon which the Christian church has been established: Jesus Christ was 100 per cent divine and 100 per cent human. We will look at the "divine" side of the equation later, but for now, let's explore why this question mattered, and ways we can know that Jesus was fully human.

It matters because for God – who created us – to rescue us, he would need to deal with the issue of our sinfulness at its very root. In the creation narrative, we are taught that once our ancestors had chosen to turn their back on God's advice and live according to their own agenda, they passed that tendency and attitude on to all of their offspring. Think of it as a moral "gene" of independence and selfishness, if you like. Every human being carries the gene that makes us want to do our own thing and have our own way. Not only that, but we each willingly choose to assert our own will and manipulate situations to suit ourselves. That doesn't always happen in obvious or drastic ways such as murder or theft or deceitfulness, but we can see it in everyday life if we just stop and watch for a moment. No one teaches a child to try and manipulate their parents when they are little. No one sits down and instructs kids at school to be bullies or to lie.

Despite our best efforts to say that we are born with an inherently "good" nature, the reality is that we suit ourselves. That shouldn't be a surprise to those of us who hold to an evolutionary view of life – since it is an inherent implication of "survival of the fittest". I guess what we wouldn't all agree on was whether such a trait is wrong or sinful. But when we see the weak exploited, the kind manipulated, or the vulnerable attacked, something inherently rises in us. Whether the evidence is the ongoing demise of morals and ethics, violence in homes or schools, national prejudice, the human race's inability to live at peace with one another, or the failure of any and all political structures to properly care for the vulnerable in our society, the evidence is all around us. But what has that got to do with the *humanity* of Jesus?

For God to rescue and redeem us, he must *be one of us*. To deal with the problem in our lives, he must somehow deal with the issue at its root. It isn't enough to deal with the symptoms – our selfishness, our pride, and our prejudice. He must deal with the human state itself. God, who made us, must somehow carry the vulnerability to temptation and to sin, without that vulnerability overwhelming him. He must find a way of *becoming human*, with all of its limitations and curtailments, while at the same time not being consumed by the human condition. The only way for God to do that is to inhabit humanity somehow. That is what happens in Jesus: God takes on human flesh. God's Son takes on humanity by being carried in the womb of a woman and born of her.

The Bible gives us a great deal of evidence of the humanity of Jesus. He grew up as a boy. He had to be educated. He learned to be a carpenter. He got tired and hungry and angry. He went to parties. He needed sleep. He ate meals with friends. He drank wine. When he was beaten and tortured as a man he bled, felt pain, and died. He had emotions of sadness when his friend died. All of these indicate the utter humanity of Jesus. And with his humanity comes vulnerability. There is no clearer picture of that vulnerability and that humanity than the picture of his young mother, Mary, giving birth to him. This was a real birth with real labour pains for Mary and real trauma for Jesus. And after he was born, she wrapped him in swaddling cloths to keep him warm, and she no doubt breastfed him to look after him. God came *in flesh* because it was the only way to redeem us without *dehumanizing* us. In order to rescue humanity, he had to enter humanity.

Prayer

Lord,
What does it mean that you became human for me?
How far did you limit yourself? I do not know, because it was such an act of humility.
Would you limit your understanding for me?
Would you limit your wealth and power for me?
What did it feel like to be curtailed to one place, one moment in history and time?
Help me to understand that in order to reach all of humanity, you had to become one human being.
Give me the ability to understand that this limitation was essential if the problem of sin were to be addressed.
Thank you that your humanity takes you beyond the realms of a God who is distant, and brings you close.
You become the God who is here, present, and experiencing life with all of its limitations and challenges.
Your humanity separates the way you deal with the world from all other traditions and religions.
Your humanity tells me you not only understand suffering; you also experience it.
Your humanity tells me you not only understand temptation; you were also confronted with it as a reality in your life.
In your humanity, you not only bring God to me, but you also show me what being truly human really means.
Thank you that you understand.
Thank you that you came to us when we could not come to you.
Thank you that you care so much that you would leave heaven for us.
Help me to worship you.
Amen.

DAY 5

The Messiah

Andrew, Simon Peter's brother, was one of the two who heard what John had said and who had followed Jesus. The first thing Andrew did was to find his brother Simon and tell him, "We have found the Messiah" (that is, the Christ). And he brought him to Jesus.

John 1:40–42 (NIV)

The woman said, "I know that Messiah" (called Christ) "is coming. When he comes, he will explain everything to us."

Then Jesus declared, "I, the one speaking to you – I am he."

John 4:25–26 (NIV)

Israel knows what it means to suffer oppression. In almost every generation there have been those who have shown their hatred of the Jewish race. Jewish men and women have been retained in ghettos, concentration camps, or prisons. The Old Testament and the New Testament speak of a great deal of persecution and attack against the Jews as well. They were enslaved by the Egyptians and taken into captivity by the Assyrians, the Babylonians, and the Persians. In the time between the Old and the New Testaments they were dominated by the Roman Empire. As a result, deep within the Jewish psyche there was a longing that God would deliver on his promise to provide someone who would lead them out of domination by a foreign power and into freedom to be their own people in their own land, free to worship God. This was their longing for a Messiah.

God had promised the Jews that he would raise up a deliverer for them, someone who would rescue them and be a figurehead for their liberation. The transliterated Jewish form of the word that describes this person is "Messiah"; the Greek form of the same title is "Christ". Their expectation, by the time of the birth of Jesus, was of someone who would lead them in military conflict and who would drive out foreign occupiers, thus freeing them from the Roman tyrants. This was a deeply embedded form of understanding of their deliverer, so it is hardly surprising that many of them found it difficult to understand Jesus as their Messiah. Yet some of those alive during Jesus' earthly ministry recognized him as their longed-for rescuer. Andrew – a fisherman – and the other apostles came to see Jesus as the Messiah they had hoped for. Yet even they continually struggled to understand the kind of liberation Jesus was bringing. They repeatedly assumed that he was a revolutionary who would overthrow the Romans. Even after Jesus' death and resurrection, they were confused about whether his kingdom was fundamentally a political one or a spiritual one.

Jesus was their Messiah, but not the kind of Messiah they had anticipated. In his exchange with a woman at a well, she clearly spoke of the Samaritan longing for the Messiah too (the Samaritans were a half-race of Jews who were despised by the Jews, and vice versa). Jesus clearly identified himself as the Messiah that she was longing for. Many people, including Christians, are surprised by the frankness of Jesus' self-identification as the Messiah. Perhaps that is because we are less fluent in the Bible story itself, or perhaps it is because we, too, want a different kind of deliverer?

Jesus the Messiah (Jesus Christ) came in peace to establish a kingdom reign and rule of God in which true freedom would be found by forgiveness and by learning the lessons of humility, openness to God, and forgiveness. He did not come in power and might, with weapons and armies. He came in peace. Yet he did overturn the political and religious structures that oppressed the Jews. He showed them how to be liberated from the oppression of Rome by rediscovering their dignity, asserting their equality, and challenging the unfair practices of the oppressor.

Jesus is our Messiah, too – our rescuer. He liberates us from sin and from wrong influences and from a wrong view of ourselves. We still find ourselves in a world of struggle, though. We still face challenges. Perhaps we, too, have a wrong idea of what our rescuer has come to do for us?

Prayer

Lord,

Help us to understand the way in which you have sent your Son to rescue us.

Forgive us when we turn the Lord Jesus Christ into some kind of easy fix or quick answer.

Forgive us when we think that following our Messiah means we will never struggle or face oppression or difficulty.

Forgive us when we turn faith in Christ into a currency by which we seek to buy an easy life.

Help us to understand the power of the deliverance that Christ brings into our lives.

Help us to receive deliverance from sin.

Help us to receive deliverance from wrong thinking about ourselves and about others.

Help us to understand that when we have been freed by the Son, we are free indeed.

We pray for those who are facing oppression around the world, particularly for those Christians who need to know that you are with them and that they are not alone.

Comfort them.

Strengthen them.

Surround them.

And we pray for the peace of Jerusalem and for the Jewish people. Thank you for your love for them. Turn the hearts of many to the Messiah, Yeshua. Let them see him clearly and receive his gift of deliverance for them.

Amen.

DAY *6*

God's Only Son

For this is how God loved the world: He gave his one and only Son, so that everyone who believes in him will not perish but have eternal life. God sent his Son into the world not to judge the world, but to save the world through him.

John 3:16–17 (NLT)

The Bible makes startling claims about Jesus. To many modern people, these claims are offensive and difficult to accept. Yet the fact remains that the Jesus of the New Testament has a unique identity, mission, and call.

The Bible teaches that Jesus is the one and only Son of God. There is no other. That is because Jesus alone carries humanity and divinity in one person. As we will see shortly, he was "conceived by the Holy Spirit" and born of the Virgin Mary. As such, he is the unique revelation of God to humanity.

All of God's redemptive purposes and plans coalesce in the life, ministry, and sacrifice of Jesus Christ. He alone can pay the price for sin. He alone can reveal the Father to us. He alone fulfils the prophecies and promises of Israel. He alone is the sin-bearer.

He alone is a perfect High Priest. He alone is the sacrifice that fulfils the demands of a holy God. His name is the only name, given to people, by which salvation can come. Authentic New Testament Christianity leaves no option for pluralism, where Jesus is one of a number of ways to know God. Instead it paints a picture of an exclusive Jesus whose death may be sufficient for all but is only efficient in those who believe in him and call upon his name.

Jesus had this understanding of himself, too. The exchange that led to the words of John 3:16–17 took place with a leading Jewish rabbi called Nicodemus. Jesus was challenging the Jewish ideas of who God was and what he was like with his words, just as he challenges modern people. Later in the same Gospel, Jesus, speaking about himself, told his disciples that he was the only Way, the only Truth and the only Life (John 14:6). In fact, John repeatedly has Jesus telling his followers about the unique and distinct ways in which Jesus brings God to men and women. The whole of New Testament spirituality hangs on this remarkable claim – that Jesus Christ was the unique, full, and final revelation of God to humanity. This one man has brought redemption to the world. He has reversed the curse of Adam and has made forgiveness, new birth, and new life possible.

If we want to know what God is like, we look at Jesus. If we want to see how God deals with us, we look at how Jesus deals with people. If we want to understand the words of Scripture, we interpret them through the lens of Jesus. He makes sense of the Law, the Prophets and everything else in the Bible. He is the subject behind the whole of Scripture, and when a Christian preacher opens the Bible to try and explain its meaning to others, Jesus must be the centre of her or his thinking.

This uniqueness has always been difficult for those who are not Christians. Yet Jesus himself does not leave us with other options. He does not give us the option of making him simply another pathway to God. He does not permit us to view him as just a good teacher, an interesting miracle worker, or a high-calibre moral example. When he encountered people during his earthly ministry, he called them to leave everything and to follow him. He disrupted their lives with his demand for total commitment. He did not let them choose him when it was convenient.

He may have called himself their friend, their brother, and their fellow Jew, but he also showed them that he was their Lord.

The same unique identity and demands rest with him today. He is still the only way.

Prayer

Lord,

Forgive me when I rank you alongside other options and hobbies.

Forgive me when I try to make you fit into my life instead of recognizing that you call me to fit into your plans and purposes.

Forgive me when I am embarrassed by the exclusiveness of your claims about yourself. I sometimes find it hard to explain your uniqueness to those from other faith traditions. Help me to find ways of being faithful to your identity that do not cause unnecessary offence, but do not let me fall into the trap of explaining your uniqueness away.

Help me never to apologize for you or be embarrassed by you again, because you have never apologized for me and you are never embarrassed by me.

Forgive me when I put something else at the centre of Christianity instead of letting you be at the centre of my faith.

Help me not to replace you with a watered-down version of who you are.

Above all, thank you that you came into the world so that the world might be rescued and so that people might know your Father.

Thank you that I have eternal life because I believe in you.

Thank you that your desire is to bring many men and women into your kingdom.

Thank you for your unique work in my life and the lives of all who trust in you.

Amen.

DAY 7

Our Lord

Therefore God also highly exalted him
and gave him the name
that is above every name,
so that at the name of Jesus
every knee should bend,
in heaven and on earth and under the earth,
and every tongue should confess
that Jesus Christ is Lord,
to the glory of God the Father.

Philippians 2:9–11

Some years ago there was a phrase that was popular in Christian circles. It went something like this: *Jesus may be your Saviour – but is he your Lord?* I've never really understood how the two could be separated.

You see, to recognize that Jesus is the Saviour of the world and to invite him to be *your* Saviour is to invite him to take over the reins of your life and to give him control. One of the greatest threats to Christian faith today, and one of the reasons why there is so much apathy in the church, lies in the fact that many Christians think it is possible to have Jesus as their Saviour *without* making him their Lord. That is just not possible.

One of the most frequently used titles of Jesus in the New Testament is that of "Lord". But what does "Lordship" mean, and why does Jesus deserve such a description?

Jesus deserves to be called Lord because it is an accurate description of what he is. As we will see later, he is present in creation and he is coequal with God the Father and God the Holy Spirit. So the reality is that Jesus *is* Lord, not because we ask him to be but because this is his actual position and authority in the universe.

He also deserves to be called "Lord" because of what he has done for us. Paul, when writing to the Philippians, made it clear that Jesus has been highly exalted by his Father because Jesus was willing to take the form of a slave, to limit himself in his humanity, and to die for us. He willingly and gladly subjected himself to death upon a cross, bearing the punishment that we deserved and turning away his Father's wrath by taking it upon himself. He experienced rejection, pain, and death for us. His willingness to endure such things more than qualifies him for Lordship.

In every one of the great sermons recorded in the book of Acts, the Lordship of Jesus is not something that becomes a reality by invitation. It is a reality that is declared and boldly announced by the early church. Jesus *is* Lord.

What, then, does the Lordship of Jesus mean? There are a number of ways in which we can understand this. Firstly, it means that we are under his rule and therefore his protection.

Secondly, if he is our Lord, then we are his servants. This means that when he asks us to do something, we should do it. If he asks us to move house, then we should. When he asks us to make a sacrifice for his kingdom, we should be willing to do so. If we are faced with the choice of doing what we want or doing what Jesus wants, then we do what Jesus wants. Thirdly, as our Lord, he is responsible for us. It is his "job" to look after us.

There is a great cost to be counted when deciding whether to submit our lives to Jesus. If we lay our lives before him, then he is free to do what he wants with them. At the same time, there is a great freedom and joy in giving our lives to Jesus because he is a kind, caring, and loving Lord.

We are never entirely free. We think we are, but we are not. The alternatives to wearing the livery of Christ are either our own selfish choices or those of satan. Neither of these is as liberating an option as submitting to the Lordship of Jesus – even if they pretend to be for a little while.

Prayer

Lord,

I often try to fool myself into thinking that I am not under anyone's lordship. It does not take very long for me to realize that I am always dominated by something.

Forgive me when I allow my own personal agenda to be the thing that is lord in my life. Forgive me when I put my own needs, desires, and wants above other people's, as if I am more important than they are.

Forgive me when I allow evil to be my lord and when I

deliberately or unintentionally push others aside or manipulate them or turn away from their need.
Forgive me when I try to place myself as lord over other people in any way.
Forgive me when I behave with arrogance and pride before you.
Forgive me when I reject your Lordship over my life.
Help me to live under your rule.
Help me to trust you more.
Help me to be open to doing your will, no matter what the cost.
Help me to be willing to say "Yes" to whatever you ask of me.
Thank you that your Lordship is the best way to live and that your yoke is easy and your burden is light.
Help me to walk with you and to remain yoked to you always.
Amen.

DAY 8

Conceived by the Holy Spirit

Now the birth of Jesus Christ took place in this way. When his mother Mary had been betrothed to Joseph, before they came together she was found to be with child from the Holy Spirit. And her husband Joseph, being a just man and unwilling to put her to shame, resolved to divorce her quietly. But as he considered these things, behold, an angel of the Lord appeared to him in a dream, saying, "Joseph, son of David, do not fear to take Mary as your wife, for that which is conceived in her is from the Holy Spirit."

Matthew 1:18–20 (ESV)

Jesus' paternal line comes directly from God the Father. The Bible tells us that the Holy Spirit himself implanted the seed in Mary's womb. This is important because it means that Jesus carries full divinity as well as full humanity.

His "paternity" comes directly from God the Father through the agency of God the Holy Spirit. Just as we previously explored the importance of Jesus' humanity, I now want to take a few moments to explore the importance of Jesus' divinity.

There are many important reasons for Jesus being conceived by the Holy Spirit that we could highlight. Let me explain just three very briefly.

Firstly, Jesus is able to save us because he is 100 per cent God. What good would it be to have a Messiah who was unable to rescue us? Jesus' divinity means he is able to save.

Secondly, Jesus' divinity means that he is able to show us exactly what God is like. We no longer need to try and guess God's nature. There is a story in the Old Testament where Moses asks God if Moses can see God's face. God replies that that is not possible. The remarkable thing about the divinity of Jesus is that we can now see what God is like, in the face and the life of Jesus.

Thirdly, because Jesus was conceived by the Holy Spirit, it means that Jesus was born without sin. This means that he did not inherit the attributed or inherited sin that all other human beings carry. This liberated him and enabled him to be the perfect and spotless sacrifice for our sins. It also means he did not need to make atonement for his own sin, because he had none. This then means that his priesthood is entirely different in order and magnitude to that of any of the previous high priests.

The fact that Jesus was conceived by the Holy Spirit helps us understand who he is, what God is like, and his sinless and divine nature – but we must be careful not to make the mistake of thinking that it is only the divinity of Jesus that matters. His life of perfect obedience was one that he lived *as a fully human being*. In effect, Jesus does not only show us what God is like; he also shows us what it is like to be truly human. I would argue that Jesus is the only *truly human* being ever to have lived, because the rest of us have been marred by sin. This is a great encouragement to us, because it shows us what being alive is really like, and fills us with hope for our own lives.

One last thought: while Jesus was conceived by the Holy Spirit in the womb of Mary and this was a unique event, never to be repeated, it is true to say that every time someone is born again, Jesus is born in him or her by the power of the Holy Spirit. Of course this is not another incarnation, but it is the same Holy Spirit causing Jesus to be born in us, so that the world might see him through us.

Prayer

Lord,
Thank you for the way in which you gave us your Son.
Thank you that Jesus shows us what you are like and that we are not left having to guess.
Thank you that Jesus brings you to us, and thank you that he brings us to you.
Thank you that Jesus has the power to rescue us and to make atonement for our sin, precisely because he carries both your nature and ours.
Thank you that the spotless, sinless Lamb of God was willing to die for me.
Thank you that the same Holy Spirit births Christ in all those who call upon you in repentance and humility.
Thank you for the gift of forgiveness and life you offer us through your Son.
Amen.

DAY *9*

Born of the Virgin Mary

"Behold, the virgin shall conceive and bear a son,
and they shall call his name Immanuel."

Matthew 1:23; Isaiah 7:14 (ESV)

And Mary said to the angel, "How will this be, since I am a virgin?"

Luke 1:34 (ESV)

In Isaiah 7:14, the word translated as "virgin" in our Bibles actually means "young woman". Some people argue that this means the idea of Mary being a virgin doesn't really matter. Yet in Matthew 1 and Luke 1 the words used are clearly intended to present the idea of virginity. So does it matter, and if so, why does it matter, and what does it actually mean?

Let's start with what it actually means, as there can be some confusion about this. Some parts of the church believe that Mary's virginity is perpetual – that is to say that she never had intercourse or bore other children, even after Jesus' birth. It is hard to see this in the Bible, as it seems clear that Mary and Joseph had intercourse *after* the birth of Jesus. Indeed, there are a number of places in the Bible that mention Jesus' brothers and sisters (e.g. Matthew 12:46; 13:55–56; Luke 8:19).

Secondly, the virginity of Mary does not mean that she was sinless. She was a very special woman, and it is right that we should treat her with respect, but there is no indication in the Bible that she is to be worshipped. Indeed, she tried to persuade her Son to perform a miracle before his time (John 2:1–5), and she tried to distract him from his ministry later on (Mark 3:31–34). She was special, but she was not perfect.

So what does the virgin birth mean, and why does it matter? It means that Jesus was born of Mary by the Holy Spirit's immediate and direct intervention in Mary's womb. No sexual intercourse was involved, and therefore no man. The clear and simple reason for this is that Jesus needed to carry complete divinity, as explored in Reflection 8. Had intercourse been involved, Jesus would have carried purely human, and therefore fallen, DNA.

The absence of sexual intercourse ensures the complete divinity of Christ and demonstrates that to Mary, to Joseph, and to the wider world in time. It does NOT mean that sexual intercourse between a man and a woman is inherently wrong or sinful. That is a complete fallacy. Sexual intimacy between a husband and wife is a gift of God that demonstrates and enables completeness and a joining together of the aspects of the image of God that are carried in a man and a woman.

The virgin birth is the miraculous means by which God enables Jesus to carry two complete natures – 100 per cent divine and 100 per cent human. Without this remarkable truth,

our Saviour would not be equipped to rescue us and lift us to God or to bring God to us.

Prayer

Lord,

There is a deep mystery about the virgin birth that defies explanation. I would be lying if I said I understood it completely.

Thank you for the important things that this remarkable event shows me, however.

Thank you that your Son carries my human nature and that he carries your divine nature.

Thank you that he is therefore able to understand my situation, and me, and that he is also able to rescue me from it.

Thank you that I have a perfect Mediator in Jesus.

Thank you that I have a perfect Saviour in Jesus.

Thank you that I have a perfect High Priest in Jesus.

Thank you that Jesus satisfies your demands for a holy sacrifice and that he represents me perfectly before you, and that I can therefore approach you with boldness and confidence.

Amen.

DAY *10*

The Promised King

Nathanael replied, "Rabbi, you are the Son of God! You are the King of Israel!"

John 1:49

Jesus Christ came to establish God's kingdom upon the earth. This means he came to demonstrate the rule and the reign of God – a rule and a reign where grace is possible and hope is tangible. He does not simply come as a general of God's kingdom, however: he is the King of the kingdom.

There is some history to explore here, and some implications to unpack.

The history is that in the early years of its nationhood, Israel longed for a king like the other nations. Despite God repeatedly telling them that they did not need a king because God himself would rule them, the people of Israel belligerently told the prophet Samuel that they wanted an earthly king. God gave them what they wanted, but also warned them that they were making a disastrous choice. As a result of that choice, the nation of Israel suffered bad rule, splits, divisions, and eventually captivity.

Throughout that time, however, God remained committed to continuing as their ruler.

As with any king, there are certain aspects to God's reign. Perhaps listing a few of them will help us to think about what it means to have him as our King.

- He will never abdicate.
- He will never lose the throne.
- His word is final.
- His commands are absolute.
- His protection is total.
- His strength never fails.
- He will look after all in his kingdom.
- He is benevolent and kind, but utterly fearless in the face of attack.
- He is wise and trustworthy.
- He deals swiftly and fairly with those who oppose him.
- The vulnerable and the weak are safe in his care.
- He reigns with justice.

No earthly king can compare to King Jesus. The best of rulers are still just men and women of clay. They still stumble and fall. They still make mistakes. Jesus does not. His reign and rule are the safest and best place to be.

Prayer

Lord,

Thank you that we are subjects of the King and citizens of the kingdom.

Thank you that you have established your kingdom on the earth and that one day all pain and suffering will be eliminated.

In the meantime, help us to believe that you can demonstrate the power of the kingdom in our communities of faith, and help us to continue to call out to you for tangible, visible demonstrations of your kingdom's power.

Lord, give us the faith to believe that we can do what you have called us to do:

To heal the sick.

To raise the dead.

To confront and command demons to flee.

To overcome the evil one.

Lord, let your kingdom come; let your will be done on earth as it is in heaven.

And help us to remember that in the midst of pain and confusion and hurt, you are still present.

You are our King, and we kneel before you.

Amen.

DAY 11

Fulfilled the Scriptures

"Do not think that I have come to abolish the Law or the Prophets; I have not come to abolish them but to fulfill them."

Matthew 5:17 (NIV)

For all of God's promises have been fulfilled in Christ with a resounding "Yes!" And through Christ, our "Amen" (which means "Yes") ascends to God for his glory.

2 Corinthians 1:20 (NLT)

One of the greatest threats to Christian faith today is the idea that we can separate Jesus from the Bible. Many people think that we can reconstruct Jesus to make him more acceptable to our culture and less offensive. The problem is that the great challenge of what the Bible actually says about who Jesus is must shape the Jesus in whom we believe and the Jesus that we present to the world.

We are simply not free to disregard the Bible and its portrayal of Jesus.

Jesus himself refused to disregard the Hebrew Scriptures. In fact, he was very clear that he came to fulfil the Hebrew prophecies and the Torah and the Prophets, not to remove them. When Paul was recounting the apostolic message of the Gospel to the church in Corinth, he repeatedly used the phrase "according to the Scriptures" to highlight the importance of God's Word.

Jesus Christ fulfilled every single requirement of the Hebrew Bible concerning the Messiah. The statistical probability of such a reality is incalculable. There can be absolutely no doubt whatsoever that Jesus is the Messiah according to the Hebrew Scriptures. He fulfilled all of the requirements concerning his first advent. During his earthly ministry he quoted from almost every single scroll of the Hebrew Scriptures. He repeatedly referred to them. He also fulfilled all of the prophetic words concerning the suffering of God's servant. He met all the requirements of the Torah for the sacrifice, and he embodied all that God sought to do through Israel. As we await his second advent, many of the Scriptures concerning that event have already been fulfilled – some people argue that only around 20 per cent of the prophecies concerning his return are yet to be fulfilled. He will fulfil every one.

Equally importantly, we are not free to change the character of Jesus' personhood, the nature of his ministry, or the content of his message, precisely because they have been handed down to us *according to the Scriptures.* The Jesus of the New Testament is the only Jesus we have. The teaching of the Jesus of the New Testament is the only teaching we have – complete with its challenges, demands, and promises. We are not free to change it because it is not ours to change. The message of Jesus has been entrusted to us. We have a responsibility to pass on the same message to the generation that comes after us.

We dare not change it – it is too important.

Prayer

Lord,
Help me to have fresh confidence in your Word.
Your Son is the Living Word, so please help me not to diminish the ways in which your written Word shapes us, challenges us, and encourages us.
Forgive me for the neglect of the Scriptures in my own life.
Forgive me for the times when I ignore your Word and I make Jesus less than he is.
Help me, instead, to submit to your Word, as Jesus did.
Help me to obey your Word, as Jesus did.
Help me to let your Word shape my understanding of Jesus and help me to read your Word through the lens of Jesus' life and ministry.
Forgive your Church for our neglect of your Word.
Breathe new life into us so that we may once again flourish by the preaching of your Word and the praising of your name.
Amen.

DAY 12

Faithful Jew

An account of the genealogy of Jesus the Messiah, the Son of David, the son of Abraham.

Matthew 1:1

Jesus was an observant Jew.

He was brought up in a Jewish family. His family had him circumcised on the eighth day. He was schooled in the Torah, attended synagogue, participated in the life of the Temple, and attended the feasts. He never broke the commandments and he never abandoned the truth of Judaism.

Christians would do well to remember this. While we must be careful not to become people who seek to make the church of Jesus Christ a Jewish sect, we must also be careful not to ignore our Jewish cousins or to turn our backs on their suffering and their pain. There is much that shames us in our history about our mistreatment of the Jews. Our only response can be humility and repentance.

Yet Jesus did not have any time for the backbreaking legalistic demands of the Pharisees and the relentless scrutiny and hypocrisy of the scribes. He often broke their additions to the Law, particularly their over-zealous requirements concerning the sabbath. He was not afraid to challenge legalistic religious self-righteousness. He will still challenge such attitudes – whether they are in the church or anywhere else.

The fact that Jesus was a Jew should remind us that as Christians we have been grafted into the family of God. Paul tells us we are a grafted branch, and that God has not finished with the Jews yet. Indeed, we receive our Scriptures, our Saviour, and the great motifs of our salvation from the Jews.

Jesus the Jew reminds us of our need to understand him properly. To share him well today, we must understand the culture in which he lived. We must not forget that Christianity is not primarily a Western faith. It has its roots in Judaism. That does not make us Jews, but we must not ignore the Jewishness of our Saviour and the Jewish roots of our faith.

Prayer

Lord,

Forgive us for the times we have persecuted the very people who gave us our Scriptures, our Saviour, and our symbols.

We pray for the Jewish people and ask you to turn their hearts to Christ.

We recognize that Jesus broke down the middle wall of partition between Jews and Gentiles – help us not build it up again.

Help us to understand the context and culture of Jesus' life and ministry, that we might better communicate him to those around us.

Thank you that in the new heavens and the new earth, the saints will be all those who have trusted in your Son, from the Jewish people and from the Gentile world.
Help us to avoid legalism, judgmentalism, and self-righteousness in our own attitudes and in our own church families.
Deliver us from the tight grip of legalistic fear, and help us to live freely under the fresh air of your grace and your power.
Forgive us when we have judged others too harshly – help us to mirror Jesus by fulfilling your Law by the power of your Spirit, but refusing to add legalistic minutiae to it.
Let us live in freedom.
Amen.

DAY 13

Sinless Life

You know that he was revealed to take away sins, and in him there is no sin.

I John 3:5

For our sake he made him to be sin who knew no sin, so that in him we might become the righteousness of God.

2 Corinthians 5:21 (ESV)

For Jesus to deal with the barriers that separate us from God, those same barriers must not be present in his life. That is why he had to be sinless. Since we are separated from God by sin, we need someone who is not separated from God by sin to deal with the issue that created that separation in the first place. This is important on a number of fronts. Let me outline just five.

Firstly, since Jesus acts as our High Priest, there must be nothing that creates a hindrance to his functioning in that office. Secondly, since Jesus also acts as our Sacrificial Lamb, he must be free from any of the blemishes that would make his sacrifice unacceptable. Thirdly, we need a Saviour who has faced the same challenges as we have but who has actually had the power to overcome those challenges instead of being defeated by them. Fourthly, sin gives the enemy of our lives, satan, a foothold in our lives. If Jesus were to have given that kind of foothold to the enemy, his whole ministry would have been destroyed. Fifthly and lastly, the absence of sin in the life of Jesus means that his obedience to his Father was complete and their communion uninterrupted.

That makes it all the more remarkable that the Bible tells us that Jesus not only bore our sins when he died upon the cross, but that he actually *became* sin for us. Up to this point there had never been the slightest division between the various aspects of the Godhead. God the Father, God the Son, and God the Holy Spirit had remained in perfect communion with one another. But at the point where the sinless Son of God becomes sin for us, a divine exchange takes place upon the cross. God the Father *must* turn away from his Son. In that moment, all the sin of the world is borne by Jesus. God's wrath and punishment for sin is poured out upon his own Son. All the wrongdoing in the course of history is placed on Jesus' shoulders and its weight is carried.

At the same time, the grace, life, mercy, and hope of God become available to us. God's very righteousness is available to all who will call upon the Name of Jesus and recognize their need of him. If we are genuinely willing to repent – that means to turn away from our wrongs, recognize our need of God's grace, and seek to walk in his way and his power – then God has already dealt with the sin that separated us from him. He allowed his

Son, who knew no sin, to become sin for us so that through his Son, we might become the righteousness of God.

Here is another, mind-blowing way of saying the same thing. When we turn from our own selfish and sinful ways and look to Jesus Christ on the cross, and when we genuinely repent, we realize that God has *placed our sin and its punishment* upon his Son, and God has placed *his Son's righteousness and holiness* upon us. He welcomes us into his family and he treats us as his children, because that is what we have become. Jesus has dealt with our separation by allowing himself to be separated. He has conquered the very thing that conquered us.

Prayer

Lord,

The fact that your Son was sinless seems so incredible. How can any person be perfect? Yet for him to be the Saviour we need, he had to be perfect.

Thank you that his divinity and his humanity link him to you and to us and that his perfection and sinlessness perfectly qualify him to be our Redeemer.

I do not know what to say to you in response to the fact that your Son bore my sin on the cross, despite the fact that he was sinless. It leaves me speechless to think that you have allowed your Son to bear my sin and that you have shared your righteousness with me.

I do not deserve such love, and I do not feel worthy of such extravagant grace, but I recognize that without it, I have no ground upon which to stand before you.

Help me to live for you with a fresh sense of acceptance

of your grace for me. Your gift to me, in your Son, is inestimable, but I thank you for it.

May I show forgiveness to others just as you have shown forgiveness to me, and may I find grace each day to start afresh, knowing just how much you love me and how much you have been willing to give for me.

Amen.

DAY *14*

Friend of Sinners

Now all the tax collectors and sinners were coming near to listen to him. And the Pharisees and the scribes were grumbling and saying, "This fellow welcomes sinners and eats with them."

Luke 15:1–2

It is one thing to have been sinless and to have borne our sin in his own body and upon the cross, but Jesus actually enjoyed spending time with people who were broken and forgotten by the religious society of his day. He liked hanging out with people like you and me.

This annoyed the religious people around him a great deal. They didn't really understand why Jesus would spend time with people whom the religious leaders thought were unacceptable. Many of the people with whom Jesus spent time were considered to be social outcasts – yet he went to them nevertheless. He spent time with prostitutes, tax collectors, liars, lepers, and Samaritans. Not only that; he also spent time with those whose position in society meant that they were considered to be less important.

Among his friends were women and children. Jesus was not afraid to break social norms, or to cut through some of the man-made taboos and restrictions that people had placed on others.

We see throughout Jesus' ministry the way God reaches out to those on the edge of society. When his birth took place, it was announced to shepherds, who were considered untrustworthy and unreliable. Yet they were among the first people to worship him. As a baby, he found his home in a stable, then as a refugee. He touched lepers, he raised the dead, and he allowed people whose conditions meant they should be locked away from society to come close to him and to touch him. He knew these people by name – they were not vague and far away. They were called Mary or Zacchaeus or Lazarus.

It is an interesting exercise to compare the life and ministry of John the Baptist, Jesus' cousin, to the life and ministry of Jesus himself. John was really the last of the Old Testament prophets. He was also a Nazirite, which meant he could not touch the dead, drink alcohol, or break a series of restrictions placed upon him by his vows. John could not have been with a leper; Jesus healed them. John could not have mixed with prostitutes and tax collectors; Jesus spent time with them and enjoyed their company. John could not have gone anywhere near a Samaritan, let alone a Samaritan woman, but Jesus spent an afternoon talking to one, and they drank water together. John could not have drunk wine; Jesus turned water into wine. The differences between the two men are stark – and important.

As Christians, we too often behave like John the Baptist, separating ourselves from those whom we consider to be less holy than we are because we fear they may pollute us. Jesus had a very different view. He knew that his company infused those around him with hope and grace. Love is always stronger than hate. Grace is always stronger than legalism. Acceptance is always stronger than rejection.

If Jesus accepted us, how much more must we learn to welcome and accept others – even when we fundamentally disagree with their lifestyle choices? Acceptance comes before change is possible – it can never be conditional.

Prayer

Lord,
Thank you that your Son, Jesus, spent time with sinners.
Thank you that he refused to be separated from the people who really needed him.
Thank you that he still spends time with broken and failed people like me.
Thank you that you accept me before you change me, and that in discovering your acceptance I am given the grace and the power to change.
Help me to model that same love and grace and acceptance to others.
Deliver me from religious legalism and elitism.
Remind me of all that Christ has done for me in accepting me, and help me to treat other people in the same way.
Amen.

DAY 15

The Teacher

"Lord, to whom would we go? You have the words that give eternal life."

John 6:68 (GNB)

Jesus taught with his words, his actions, and his responses. He was the greatest preacher ever to have lived. His words bring life to those who hear them and heed them. When he speaks, it is like arrows of light piercing the darkness.

The very first of Jesus' words that we have recorded are those he spoke when he was separated from his mother and his earthly father as a boy. They had been travelling, and Jesus became detached from Mary and Joseph. Eventually they found him in the Temple, and when they questioned him about where he had gone, he asked them where they thought he would be – didn't they realize he would be about his Father's business? (Luke 2:41–52)

Throughout his life and ministry, Jesus' words captivated people. Again and again he gathered crowds when he sat down to speak with them. At the centre of his teaching were simple stories. He told stories about bread, about birds, and about boats. He talked about building houses, farming fields, and gathering wheat. His language was accessible and his words were simple. Yet the truths he taught were life changing and profound. His parables left people scratching their heads, and he often used metaphors and similes that needed time to grow in the minds and thinking of his listeners. Yet the truth of what he said transformed lives. There are a number of reasons for that.

Firstly, Jesus did not only speak the truth: Jesus *is* the Truth. We have become so used to the idea that truth is a statement that we are taken aback when we realize that truth is actually a Person and his name is Jesus. I can know facts and statistics about Jesus and they can be true, but they pale into insignificance when I actually get to know Jesus. I have known him for almost thirty years and have only just scratched the surface of what he is like.

Secondly, Jesus not only spoke the truth; he also demonstrated it. His words, his actions, and his attitudes perfectly matched. This gave his teaching such authority that many around him commented on it. They had heard other preachers and teachers before, but none like Jesus. Jesus not only said things that were true; he also demonstrated things that were true by raising the dead, healing the sick, and delivering people from demons.

Lastly, Jesus was not afraid to confront people with the truth. Whether that be a religious leader who thought he was above question, a wealthy man who thought he had everything sorted out, or a woman who was running away from the truth of her immoral life, Jesus made the truth accessible. He made the truth make sense.

And where did all of this wisdom and truth come from? The answer is clear. Jesus repeatedly quoted the Hebrew Bible and he was grounded in a solid and unmovable relationship with his Father. Jesus spent time in prayer, in worship, and in study.

His words have continued to change lives. His truths have shaped cultures, given hope to billions of people and changed the course of history. His teaching has toppled empires, inspired movements, and liberated those who have been oppressed. There has never been, and there will never be, a more adept, brilliant, and relevant teacher than Jesus.

Prayer

Lord,
Help me to sit at your feet and listen to your words.
I so often find myself tempted to rush around and do other things because those other things can appear to be so very, very important.
Help me to hear the words of life again as I listen to you through the Scriptures.
Teach me, O Teacher, the difference between right and wrong.
Teach me, O Teacher, how to live with God at the centre of my decisions, my intentions, and my attitudes.
Teach me to listen to you.
Teach me to honour you.
Teach me to obey you.
Please help me to live a life that is authentic, where what I say, what I think, and what I do are deeply connected.
Forgive me when I think I know more than you or when I pretend not to understand you because your words are too

challenging and your commands too hard.
And help me, Lord, to speak in such a way that I will teach others about you. Help me to mimic you to others.
Help me to learn a little more every day and to become more like you with each season of my life.
Amen.

DAY *16*

The Saviour

And we have seen and do testify that the Father has sent his Son as the Savior of the world

1 John 4:14

There have been many wonderful teachers in the history of the world – although none as wonderful as Jesus. There has only ever been one Saviour. Jesus Christ did not come simply to teach us. He did not come simply to set a wonderful example. He came to seek and to save those who were lost.

The word "Saviour" is one of the most commonly used nouns to describe who Jesus is and what he came to do – but what does it mean?

The Greek word for Saviour has a number of meanings. Let me explain three of them.

Firstly, it means to rescue from a life-and-death situation. Like a lifeguard rescuing someone who is drowning, Jesus is the Saviour who rescues us from the life-and-death consequences of sin and our own foolishness.

Secondly, the idea of salvation is connected with being set free from a force or a power that is much stronger than we are. In this context it means deliverance. Jesus is our Saviour in this sense because he delivers us from the grip and the power of evil in general and from satan in particular. Jesus is stronger than any other force or power and is therefore able to rescue us from those forces. He is our Deliverer.

Thirdly, the idea of Jesus as our Saviour is linked to the idea of healing. To save someone is also to set them free from suffering and from pain. To save someone in this sense is to heal them. Jesus is our spiritual healer because he has paid the price for our sin and he is able to apply the balm of his grace to the wounds of our pride and broken lives. He is still in the business of healing today. Sometimes he does it through doctors and nurses and sometimes he does it through miracles, but he is still a healing God. Sometimes he heals us through death, after which all pain and suffering is removed from the life of a Christian forever.

Here is one final way of looking at the saving power of Jesus. He has saved us from the penalty of sin because he has taken that penalty upon himself. He has also saved us from the power of sin because he has given us the ability to resist temptation. One day, however, he will save us from the very presence of sin, and we will no longer be allured by its temptations.

When I think of Jesus as my Saviour, it moves me very deeply. Perhaps that is because I am aware of how much he has forgiven in my life, or because I know how many times I have let him down and yet he has come to my rescue.

We Christians often make the mistake of thinking that Jesus is only *our* Saviour, though. The Bible tells us he is much more than this. He is the Saviour of the world. One day the very fabric of the earth will be made new. His salvation affects us personally, but it also affects the structures of the world and the substance of the earth.

Hallelujah, what a Saviour!

Prayer

Lord,
I cannot begin to express my gratitude to you for what you have done for me.
Thank you for rescuing me from the dangers of my selfishness and my pride.
Thank you for rescuing me from the powers that are stronger than me.
Thank you for healing me of my sin and for the many times you have healed those who are physically, emotionally, or relationally sick.
Thank you that you have carried the penalty of my sin.
Thank you that you have given me the power to overcome sin.
Thank you that you will one day remove the very presence of sin.
Thank you that you are at work in the world and that you are the Saviour of the world.
Thank you for your incredible patience with me.
Help me to walk daily in your forgiveness, to accept it afresh every morning, and to live in the freedom and joy of knowing that you are my Rescuer, my Redeemer, and my Saviour.

Help me to share your saving love with others around me, and forgive me when I selfishly want you to be my Saviour and no one else's.
May my life reflect your saving grace to others.
Amen.

DAY 17

The Healer

That evening, at sunset, they brought to him all who were sick or possessed with demons. And the whole city was gathered around the door. And he cured many who were sick with various diseases, and cast out many demons; and he would not permit the demons to speak, because they knew him.

Mark 1:32–34

There are many Christians in the church who hold to what they describe as the "Foursquare Gospel". That means they believe in Jesus as the Saviour, the Healer, the Baptizer in the Holy Spirit, and the Coming King. I have picked up each one of these in individual reflections.

I would like to take a few moments now to think about Jesus as the Healer.

That Jesus healed people during his earthly ministry is obvious. He healed the sick. He raised the dead. He set people free from demonic control. These actions demonstrated to those around him that God's kingdom had come in a new and fresh way through Jesus, and they enabled many to hear the message of salvation and forgiveness and the kingdom that Jesus brought. In John's record of Jesus' earthly ministry, he refers to some of these healings as "signs" that point to who Jesus is, why Jesus came, and what Jesus does. In chapter 8 of Matthew's record of Jesus' earthly ministry, Matthew tells us that Jesus healed many people in different contexts. Matthew goes on to say that Jesus did this so that the words of Isaiah 53 might be fulfilled: "He took our infirmities and bore our diseases."

There is some controversy about whether or not physical healing is still operational in the church today. Some Christians believe that this gift ceased with the finalization of the New Testament. I do not agree. In the pages of the New Testament Jesus was undoubtedly a great healer. And my interpretation of the Bible is that God continues to heal people today.

Sometimes Jesus healed people in response to their faith. Sometimes he healed people in response to someone else's faith. Sometimes he healed people and faith is not mentioned at all. What is clear is that the Jesus of the Gospels was Someone who was known as a great Healer.

Now, this same Jesus is still alive and well in heaven. He has not lost any of his powers. He is, therefore, still able to heal. There are many who can tell stories of Jesus' healing power in their lives. I am one of them. I encountered the healing power of Jesus in my own physical body a number of years ago. As a church, we regularly pray for sick people to be healed and we see healings take place as we ask Jesus to touch them.

There remains a great mystery about healing. I have prayed for many people who have not been healed in this life – they have continued to live with their condition or they have died. Yet I still believe that Jesus is a healer. Why?

Firstly, the greatest healing a person can experience is the healing of their soul through the forgiveness of sins. Jesus continues to bring this healing to millions of people around the world every year. Indeed, you cannot be a Christian without having experienced this. Secondly, while Jesus does heal people in this life, the Christian view of death is that it is also a gateway into ultimate and final healing. All physical healings that take place before death are temporary because we go on to die. Yet those who have died in Christ are completely and permanently healed. They are more alive than they have ever been. They are more themselves than they have ever been, and they are utterly free from all pain and suffering. In every way, this is a picture of the deepest healing possible. Of course, I want people to be healed by Jesus on this side of heaven, but sometimes he chooses to bring a person into complete and full healing by bringing them to himself, and sometimes he chooses to heal them in this life. Either way, he is still a healer. Still, the most wonderful healing of all is the new life we have with him when we come to faith in Christ.

Prayer

Lord,

Thank you that you have the power to heal my sin and restore me to right relationship with yourself.

Thank you that you have the power to remove sickness and suffering, too.

I pray for those whom I know at this moment who need your touch of healing. Would you please give them your strength. I come boldly into your presence and ask you to move in their lives that they might be restored to full health and strength.

I pray for those who are physically sick…

I pray for those who are emotionally in need of restoration…

I pray for those who are mentally ill…

I pray for those who are approaching death. Would you give them hope and confidence that as they pass through the veil of death, if they trust in you, they will enter their complete and final and eternal healing and rest. Give them and their families faith and confidence and trust at this difficult time.

I confess that I do not always understand your reasons for healing some people in this life and others in death. Help me not to excuse away the absence of healing in the church today, but help me also to be your voice and hands and heart of healing to those around me.

Thank you that Jesus is the same yesterday, today, and forever, and that nothing is impossible with him.

In every situation, keep my eyes fixed steadfastly upon him because I know that he is good and his love endures forever.

Amen.

DAY 18

He Suffered

Although he was a son, he learned obedience through what he suffered.

Hebrews 5:8 (ESV)

Christ also suffered for you…

1 Peter 2:21 (ESV)

At the heart of Christianity is a deep, deep conviction that Jesus Christ suffered for us. There are no words to convey the importance of this belief in the Christian faith. It is what sets us apart from every other religious tradition. In the midst of our many questions about suffering around the world, we can lose sight of the importance of Jesus' suffering if we are not careful. We can begin to think that God does not care and that he is detached from the pain of the world. Nothing could be further from the truth.

In Christianity, unlike any other religion in the world, God comes into the midst of our suffering and our pain. He enters the arena of suffering and endures it with us. He does not stand on the sidelines and watch. He does not tell us that all suffering is our fault. When we ask him where he is when we suffer, he points to the wounds in the hands of Jesus and tells us that he suffers with us. When we ask if he understands what it feels like to lose a child, he points to the cross and the tomb and tells us that he lost his Son, too. When we ask whether he knows what it feels like to face temptation, he points to the wilderness where Jesus was tempted by the devil. When we wonder what he knows about grief and loss and the death of a loved one, he reminds us that his Son stood at the graveside of a friend and wept, too.

The Bible makes it clear that Jesus suffered. He suffered emotionally, physically, and spiritually.

Jesus endured great rejection, misunderstanding, and ridicule. He was falsely accused and maligned. He knows what it feels like to be rejected by those he loved.

Jesus endured great pain through flogging, whipping, and beating. He had nails driven through his hands and his feet and a spear thrust into his side. He was forced to carry a heavy Roman cross and then made to endure one of the worst forms of torture and death the world has ever known.

Jesus knows what it is to be hungry, to be thirsty, and to be poor. He had no home of his own and he lived a life of solitude and celibacy. He never had any children and he never had someone to come home to with whom he could share the concerns and worries of the day.

Jesus endured great spiritual suffering. He was tempted more than we could ever understand and he was constantly under pressure to deny his faith, deny his mission, and turn away from the purpose his Father had for him. The night before his death, he was under such pressure that his sweat was mingled with blood – that is a rare human condition that only comes about in the most extreme situations of stress and pressure.

Our God understands suffering because he partakes in it with us. He does not ignore it. When we ask him why he permits suffering, I think he sometimes looks back at us and says that he doesn't just permit it; he endures it. He does not answer our question with a trite explanation. Instead, he points to his Son, he points to his own wounded heart, and he points to the world and he tells us that he carries our suffering with us. Jesus does not theologize about suffering; he shares it.

Prayer.

Lord,

I have so many questions about suffering that there are times when they crowd out my joy. I do not understand it.

I lift to you all those I know who are suffering at the moment. Please give them strength. Would you draw alongside them and whisper their name. Would you remind them that you carry the load with them. Would you help them to realize that they are not alone.

Suffering God, thank you that you do not stand watching us in our pain. Thank you that you enter our pain with us. Thank you that you do much more than talk to us about suffering; you carry it with us. Help us to realize the comfort in that in a fresh and new way.

Thank you that you can redeem suffering. Thank you that you make sense of it. Thank you that, if we let you, the scars in our lives can speak of your victory. Thank you that suffering is a universal experience, and if we let you shine through our lives, you can touch others through our example and our faithfulness.

I pray for those around the world who are suffering now because of their faith. Thank you that you gave us a warning that we would suffer if we stood for you. Thank you that we are only walking the road that has your footprints on it.

In the midst of all our questions about suffering in our lives and in the midst of all the uncertainties we have about it, would you help us to remember that we are held in the Answer's hands.

Thank you that you wrap your arms around us and endure our pain with us, and that one day it will be removed completely. Until then, give us the grace to trust you more and to sense your presence with us more deeply.

Amen.

DAY *19*

He Challenged the Self-righteous

"You snakes, you brood of vipers! How can you escape being sentenced to hell?"

Matthew 23:33

We sometimes have a picture in our heads of a Jesus who is so gentle and kind and loving and accepting that he would not say boo to a goose. We can domesticate Jesus so much that we turn him into a bit of a nondescript person who never has any views about anything and who would never challenge anyone about their behaviour or their attitudes. We make him so accepting that anything goes, and we make him so accommodating that nothing matters. The reality couldn't be further from that idea.

It is true that Jesus went out of his way to welcome those who already thought their lives were over and that they didn't matter. He embraced these people with such tenderness and acceptance that their hearts melted. He really was a friend of sinners.

On the other hand, Jesus was scathing in his denouncement of the self-righteous. He had no time for those who claimed to know God yet lived their lives in such a way that they were driving a wedge between God and ordinary people. Jesus referred to those who trumpeted their religion and ignored the broken as a "brood of vipers" and as "whitewashed tombs" (Matthew 23:27). He challenged their self-righteous indignation and their hypocritical spiritual practices because he knew there was no life in them.

The two main camps of religiously self-righteous people in the time of Jesus' earthly ministry were the Pharisees and the scribes. These two groups delighted in their own understanding of the Torah. They believed that they were the guardians of true Judaism. They often hated one another, but they were united in their desire to keep their faith pure and free from the contamination of the sinful and the unworthy.

The scribes and the Pharisees started off with good intentions, but slowly, as the years passed, those intentions became more and more motivated by fear and less and less motivated by love. They had originally wanted to protect the Torah and to make sure the Jews remained a faithful people, but they slowly became obsessed with avoiding pollution by unfaithfulness or by disobedience. So they continually extended the Law and they added layer upon layer of definition and instruction until the weight of it all was crushing people who felt unworthy, unclean, and unwanted.

Jesus exposed the hearts of those who had become caught up in such tightly bound legalism. Who had appointed them as moral guardians? Who had given them the right to teach one thing and live another? Who had told them they were better than anyone else? Who gave them the right to build barriers between ordinary people and God? How dare they play the role of moral police and the holiness defence league! Jesus cut through their hypocrisy and their theological arguments like a warm knife through butter. And he still does.

There are so many Christians who end up taking the moral high ground with others and forget that we are called to walk alongside others, not to look down our noses at them. Jesus has no time for those who think they do not need him. He does not need someone to filter out the deserving from the undeserving. He has not appointed leaders in the church as his protectors or defenders.

We are to defend the truth of who he is and the truth of the gospel, but we must not allow ourselves to assume that we decide who gets to meet God and who does not. We may be called to help people grow as disciples, but we are not given the job of having the final say on who is a Christian and who is not. God, and God alone, knows the answer to that question. Just because someone does not fit my brand of Christianity, it does not mean that they do not know Jesus. If God calls someone son or daughter, I have no right to call them anything but brother or sister.

Prayer

Lord,
Deliver me from self-righteousness.
Never let me look down my nose at others with spiritual pride.
Please help me to remember that you embrace the broken and you welcome sinners, but you will not tolerate hypocrisy or self-righteousness.
There is nothing in me that deserves the grace and love and mercy that you have shown me. Forgive me when I think there is.
Help me to welcome people and not reject them.
Help me to enable people to see Jesus and not to become an obstacle for them.
Help me not to think that my job is to filter out the unworthy from the worthy.
Give me the grace to see you in the faces of those who have given their lives to you.
Give me the courage to speak the truth in love.
Give me the conviction to challenge wrong behaviour.
Make the church family of which I am part a community of grace and truth, of love and acceptance, as well as holiness and faithfulness.
And start the work of grace deep within my own selfish heart and life.
In Jesus' name,
Amen.

DAY 20

He Embraced the Broken

"Are you tired? Worn out? Burned out on religion? Come to me. Get away with me and you'll recover your life. I'll show you how to take a real rest. Walk with me and work with me – watch how I do it. Learn the unforced rhythms of grace. I won't lay anything heavy or ill-fitting on you. Keep company with me and you'll learn to live freely and lightly."

Matthew 11:28–30 (*The Message*)

The flipside of Jesus challenging the self-righteous is that he wholeheartedly embraced those who knew they needed his help. His words to the broken and to the outcast reverberate with hope. They pulse with life.

"Be clean," he says to a leper.

"I forgive you," he says to a woman whose marriages have fallen apart.

"I don't condemn you," he says to a woman caught in the act of adultery.

"I'll have dinner with you," he says to a hated tax collector.

"Come and be my friend and my follower," he says to a zealot.

Again and again the tenderness of Jesus towards the broken is seen. In Matthew 5, at the beginning of the Sermon on the Mount, he sits down and helps the outcasts who are listening to him to understand just how much God loves them. In the passage we have here, Jesus invites those who are burned out on religious observance and the expectations of others to come and meet with him. I do not know how many times I have returned to these words over the years since I first read them. They are so life giving.

Jesus is still the same. He still invites those who are caught in the religious treadmill to come and find him. He still looks for those who think they are not good enough. He sometimes meets them in church. Sometimes he meets them in their office. He sometimes meets them as they slip out of a bedroom thinking no one has seen them. He stands beside them as they close their computer in shame. He listens to their telephone calls and then offers help.

He is the ultimate restoration man. He loves taking what is broken and fixing it. He loves to lift up our lives, so dirtied by our mistakes and our failures and our bad habits, and clean them with his love and grace.

If you are worried that you are beyond his care or that he cannot reach you, you're wrong. He is there. He is ready and he is waiting. He wants to protect you, nurture you, and refresh you – all you need to do is ask him. Of course, he won't leave you as he finds you. He will change you from the inside out. He'll give you a new heart so you can really live. He'll give you new eyes so you can see the world with fresh hope. He will challenge your priorities and upset your assumptions. His grace doesn't just accept you; it refashions you and gives you the strength to become what you never thought you could.

Never, ever be in any doubt about this, though: Jesus receives you where he finds you. You don't need to change to be accepted by him; you just need to be willing to let him change you once you meet him.

Prayer

Lord,
Thank you that you accepted me just where I was.
You came to me. You didn't expect me to sort my life out and get myself right before you accepted me.
Thank you that your grace for people like me is so beautiful and so transforming.
Thank you that you see more in me than I do in myself.
Thank you that you are willing to fashion me, to shape me, to teach me, and to show me what being alive really means.
Thank you that you give me a new heart, a new life, and new eyes to see the world.
Thank you that you paint the colours in my life with such hope.
Forgive me when I can't quite believe it.
Be patient with me when I lose sight of the wonder of your love.
Help me to walk with you – and to learn that I will always stumble if I try to run ahead.
Tune my spirit to the music of heaven.
Write a symphony of grace with the notes of my life.
Play the melody of grace through me so others can hear the song of your love.
Amen.

DAY 21

He is Our Strength

God is our refuge and strength,
a very present help in trouble.
Therefore we will not fear, though the earth should change,
though the foundations shake in the heart of the sea;
though its waters roar and foam,
though the mountains tremble with its tumult.

Psalm 46:1–3

Someone once told me they thought my faith in Jesus was nothing more than a crutch. They said I had only become a follower of Jesus because I was weak and needed someone or something to lean on. My reply shocked them, I think. I said that Jesus is not just my crutch; he is my lifeline! Without him I cannot live. Without his grace and mercy and strength I would not make it through a single day.

We can be very offended when people suggest that we are weak and need help. I am not offended at all. Instead, I am surprised when people think they are impenetrable, that they never need help or support. I wonder what it is that makes any human being think so proudly about themselves?

The Lord Jesus is our strength. He is the one who remains faithful even when others have deserted us. There are no words to express how much we need his strength and his power in our lives. Without him, the beautiful colours of the world fade to grey. Through him, we see with new eyes and we breathe with new assurance. His strength in us enables us to face any and every situation with confidence and with hope.

All other sources of strength fade and die away, but Jesus does not. Young men and women, once full of vigour and life and health, grow older. Their bodies wear out. Their minds become less strong. But those who trust in Christ can know the assurance that even while our bodies might wear out and our minds might struggle to stay focused, our *inner person* can become stronger and stronger. We may physically and intellectually fade sometimes, but Christ is the strength that constantly renews us, refreshes us, and revives us. This is much more than a "crutch"! This is a powerful source of hope and strength and life.

I have been a pastor for many years and I have seen the reality of Christ's strength in people's lives again and again. I have seen ordinary women and men bear great trials with the most astounding courage. I have seen weak and fearful people grow as strong as lions and as fearless as warriors in the face of death, destruction, and despair. I have also seen those who thought they were self-sufficient and courageous and invincible crumble in the face of death or despair. I have watched those who told me my faith was a crutch fall apart when they have had to face the greatest trials. I have been heartbroken as they have come face to face with their own mortality, only to realize that their self-confidence was like sinking sand.

The Lord Jesus strengthens us when the waves hit our lives. He is a fortress to whom we can run. He is not distant and remote and detached when we face great trials and difficulties. Instead he is present, right beside us. Our own strength comes and goes. Our confidence rises and falls, but Christ's grace is constant, his power is undiminished, and his presence is unchanged. Empires come and go. The great empires, powers, and rulers of the past now lie in mausoleums or in graves. The world's greatest emperors lose their power. Their monuments crumble and their statues are torn down. They become the subject of history lessons. The symbols of their wealth and power become exhibits in museums, locked in glass cabinets.

Christ's strength stands undiminished. He is not locked in a cabinet – he is alive. He is not the subject of history alone. He lives today, and while other "crutches" have broken and fallen, Jesus stands alive still, sustaining and strengthening all those who look to him. He is present with us always and his power is still the lifeline that we need.

Prayer

Lord,
Thank you that your power is available to me today.
I am sorry that I try to cope on my own and that I allow myself to think that I am self-sufficient. I am sorry that I buy into the idea that to need help is to be weak or fragile. I am sorry that I try to give the impression to others that I am strong.

Help me to live in your strength and not in my own. Remind me that you are not simply present to me to help me in moments of crisis, but that it is only in your strength that I can live well at all. Remind me that you are not my crutch but that you are my lifeline.

I pray for those who have not yet faced the challenges of their own weaknesses and frailty. Thank you that you are ready to comfort those who will turn to you. Thank you that you do not stand in arrogant detachment from those who stand in arrogant detachment from you. Lord, thank you that you are always ready to embrace all who will admit that they need your help.

I pray for a greater ability to rely on your power in my daily life. Help me to lift my eyes to you constantly through each day. Remind me that it is your grace that sustains me, Lord. Teach me the art of daily resilience through the importance of daily reliance on you.

I give you those things that I know are stronger than me – my cares, my worries, the challenges of my character that overwhelm me. I give you the situations in my life that feel like they will overcome me.

I give you the mistakes of my past…

I give you the challenges of my present…

I give you my fears for the future…

I freely and readily acknowledge that I do not have the power to live well. So please pour your grace and strength into my life.

Give me the grace to forgive and to receive forgiveness…

Give me the courage to speak the truth and to hear the truth…

Give me the ability to start again...
Give me the faith to walk through the darkest valleys and shadows today by reminding me that the shadow only exists because your light is shining upon me.
I pray for those who are held in the grip of terrible regimes and subject to tyrants, in their homes, in their communities, in their workplaces, and in their nations. Remind them that all tyrants will lose their power and that you reign forever.
Help me live in your strength today and always.
Amen.

DAY 22

He Established His Kingdom

"My kingdom is not from this world. If my kingdom were from this world, my followers would be fighting to keep me from being handed over to the Jews. But as it is, my kingdom is not from here." Pilate asked him, "So you are a king?" Jesus answered, "You say that I am a king. For this I was born, and for this I came into the world, to testify to the truth. Everyone who belongs to the truth listens to my voice." Pilate asked him, "What is truth?"

John 18:36–38

Some would argue that the Roman Empire was the greatest empire the world has ever seen. Whether that is true or not, to have one of its senior leaders confront you and hang the threat of execution over you would be a scary moment for anyone. Yet when Pontius Pilate is on the brink of passing a death sentence over Jesus, fear does not seem to distract Jesus. Pilate thinks he is the power broker in the conversation, but Jesus makes it clear that the Roman Empire is nothing compared to the kingdom of God, of which Jesus is King.

Over time, the idea of the kingdom of God has become synonymous with God himself. So when Jesus begins his public ministry he does so by announcing that the kingdom of God has come. That is not surprising, since we have already explored that he is God in flesh, and as King he has come to establish his visible kingdom. One way of looking at it is that in his earthly ministry, Jesus comes to demonstrate more clearly what he already is. It is interesting, therefore, that at the end of his ministry, the title, "The King of the Jews" is placed above Jesus as he is being crucified, and is written in the three great languages of the time for all to see. The writing may have been a cynical declaration in the eyes of many, but it was nevertheless a clear prophetic announcement of who he is.

Jesus uses different language to announce that he is the King of the kingdom. He sometimes says that the kingdom is near, he sometimes says that it has arrived, and he sometimes says that it is within his followers. In a sense, all are true. The kingdom is near because it is a dimension of God's rule and reign that is all around us. It has arrived because Jesus has come and brought the kingdom's demonstration with him. And it is in us because it is a kingdom mediated by the power and presence of God in our lives.

In another part of the Bible, the kingdom of God is described as righteousness, joy, and peace in the power of the Holy Spirit. The reality is that with the first advent of Jesus, the kingdom was established, but it is not yet fully consummated. That will happen when Christ returns.

The time between his two advents is the time in which we now find ourselves. It is a time when we still see the miraculous outworking of God's power around us, but not always. The kingdom is here, but it is still coming. It is already present, but it is not yet universally and fully experienced. Yet the King has come and has given us the assurance that he will come again.

We feel the tension of this waiting in our own lives and in the suffering world around us – but we do so knowing that the King is with us always. Even when we do not have the answers to why bad things happen, we must remember that we are always held in the Answer's loving and tender hands.

Prayer

Lord,

Let your kingdom come – let your rule and reign and what is best for your purposes happen in my life today, no matter what.

Let your will be done – wherever there is resistance to your purposes and your plans, soften hearts and change attitudes.

On earth, as it is in heaven – may our communities reflect the peace, grace, harmony, holiness, wholeness, and hope of your dwelling place.

Give us this day our daily bread – help us not to binge while others starve, and enable us to share what we have with those who have not.

And forgive us our sins – wash away our repeated attempts to put our desires, our selfish passions, and our wishes above yours.

As we forgive those who sin against us – give us grace to let go of the chains by which we control other people – whether chains of hate or chains of hurt.

And lead us not into temptation – give us the strength to resist the temptations that the devil lays at our door.
But deliver us from the evil one – help us to stand fast against the enemy of our souls, no matter how flattering or harmless he attempts to be.
For the kingdom, the power, and the glory all belong to you – we acknowledge that you are the Sovereign and that all power and glory and strength lie in your hand.
Now and for evermore,
Amen.

DAY 23

He Was Crucified

When they came to the place that is called The Skull, they crucified Jesus there with the criminals, one on his right and one on his left.

Luke 23:33

The closer we get to the crucifixion in the New Testament, the shorter the sentences become. We get the impression that the writers do not know what to say, so they give us the bare facts. Those facts are difficult to hear.

Each year, on Good Friday, Christians around the world gather to remember the day Jesus was murdered. In the church I lead, we have a very simple but deeply moving meeting. Our building is stripped of flowers and everything is plain and simple. We gather in relative silence and we listen to the story, line by line and blow by blow. We sing some songs that help us to think about the sacrifice and the death of Jesus Christ, and we eat bread and drink wine to remember his broken body and his spilled blood. There is only a ten- or fifteen-minute sermon. We allow space and time for the words of the Bible to penetrate our hearts, and we listen carefully to them. We don't mention resurrection – that will be celebrated on Easter Sunday, and then we will fill the church with light and music and colour and joy. Today is a day to remember the suffering of the Saviour. It is a day to be quiet. It is a day to weep. A day to hang our heads in grateful thanks and to worship, with tears, the One who gave his all for us. I find it one of the most moving services of the year. It grounds me and reminds me of all that Jesus did for me. I still don't understand it – but I believe it with all my heart, and it has changed my life forever.

There is no way I can express the meaning of the crucifixion to you here. Words cannot convey it. So instead of trying to explain it, I'll ask some questions that I don't have answers to either.

- What did it feel like for the disciples when it seemed that everything was falling apart?
- How could Jerusalem turn so violently against Jesus in just one week?
- How would you feel if you were innocent and yet sentenced to death, and while you were watching, someone who was guilty was set free in your place?
- How did Jesus endure the humiliation of being mocked and stripped naked and paraded like a horse for sale at a market?
- How many times did they whip Jesus before he fell to the ground in agony?
- How did he manage to carry a cross for so long after being beaten so badly?

- Did the wood dig into the wounds on his back?
- Why did only one person help him?
- Did Jesus look at the soldiers who nailed him to the cross, and if he did, what did he think?
- How did his mother feel?
- How did his Father feel?
- How, on earth, could Jesus ask his Father to forgive?
- Why did the world go dark for three hours? Was creation on the brink of collapse because its Sustainer was dying?
- How did those watching feel as the sun stopped shining?
- Could anyone love that much?
- Did he do this for me?

There is no other faith, God, or Saviour with such sacrificial love at his heart. There are no words to describe the depth of love that was shown for the world as Jesus Christ died. This is the heart of the Christian faith.

This is the cost of our redemption.
This is the extent of God's love.

Prayer

Lord,
I do not know what to say.
In silence and in tears,
I worship you.
I kiss the feet of my Saviour because my words are useless.
Amen.

DAY 24

He Bore God's Wrath

Much more surely then, now that we have been justified by his blood, will we be saved through him from the wrath of God.

Romans 5:9

There have been many attempts to understand how the cross of Jesus Christ works in our lives. Some have helped us to see the cross in new and fresh ways. The next four reflections are my attempt to understand some of the ways in which we understand the cross to have obtained our redemption.

The first, and I would argue the most central, way of understanding what Jesus did when he died for us on the cross is known as penal substitution. To modern ears this can sound offensive, and there are many who think it is a false way of viewing the death of Jesus. Yet for many others, this is the foundation of how to view the sacrifice of Jesus for us. I do not believe it to be the only lens for understanding the crucifixion, but I do understand it to be a central way of doing so.

The explanation of penal substitution is relatively straightforward. We deserve God's punishment and wrath because of our selfish and sinful choices and our selfish and sinful nature. We do not deserve God's forgiveness and grace. Jesus, on the other hand, does not deserve any punishment from his Father. Yet the holy and righteous demands of God concerning sin need to be satisfied. For that reason, when Jesus dies on the cross, he endures the wrath and punishment of God being poured out upon him for the sins of the world. By doing so, he makes the grace and love and mercy and acceptance that *he* deserves available to *us*. God the Father punishes his Son in order to release us, and his Son receives that wrath and endures that suffering so that we can be released from the power and the penalty of our sin.

This understanding lies at the heart of the way the apostle Paul explains the cross to the Romans, the Galatians, the Ephesians, the Colossians, and many others, and it sits at the heart of the way the apostles Peter and John also explain the death of their Master, Jesus.

In recent years, some of my friends and others have rejected this theory of the atonement because they think it is unfair and that only a cruel father would punish an innocent son in such a way. I think their reasoning is flawed, for a number of reasons.

Firstly, the wonder of the cross is that the Father, the Son, and the Holy Spirit all willingly enter into it. The Father is not volunteering the Son for crucifixion against the Son's will, and the Son is not demanding that the Father punish him. Instead, the Father, the Son, and the Holy Spirit enter into this act of mutual and communal suffering out of love for one another and love for the world that God has created, sustains, and longs to redeem. This is not an act of cruelty; it is an act of indescribable love and commitment.

Secondly, this is the only way that the righteous and just demands of God's own holiness can be met. God cannot treat sin lightly. If he were to do so, he would be inconsistent and the consequences of sin through the years would not make sense. Instead, the Holy Trinity determines to acknowledge the consequences and the cost of sin, but at the same time to take the consequences and pay the cost himself. God pronounces the only sentence that can be pronounced: guilty. God then takes that sentence upon himself and pays the cost of it so that others can go free.

Thirdly, without the theory of penal substitution, we are only left with the idea that God somehow has to make a deal with satan or with evil or with humanity.

The other theories of Jesus' death and the reasons for it help us to understand other reasons for the cross, but none of them deal with the issue of holiness and the actual cost and consequences of sin as deeply as this theory does. Jesus bore God's wrath upon the cross so that we did not have to. That is amazing grace.

Prayer

Lord,

The cross is a mystery.

I will never understand how it works, but thank you that you have given me some ways of approaching its meaning and significance.

Help me not to view the cross through a single lens. To do so makes it feel less beautiful and less meaningful. Instead of placing the cross behind the window of one theory, help me to see it through the diamond of several. Let its colour and light and beauty be refracted into my heart and spirit.

Forgive us when we make the cross a point of disagreement and schism. Help us find a way to discover our unity at the foot of the cross. Help us not to attack one another over how the cross works.

Please help us not to make the cross more palatable by reducing its horror. Thank you that on the cross you poured out your wrath upon your Son. Thank you, Lord Jesus, that you willingly bore our penalty. Thank you, Holy Spirit, that you strengthened the Son to endure such pain. Thank you, Father, Son, and Holy Spirit, that you were united in your love for one another and in your commitment to us to such an extent.

I come to the cross and I kneel before it, acknowledging my guilt and revelling in your forgiveness, Lord. Thank you for the divine exchange that takes place here, and for the hope and life and forgiveness that flow to me through the substitutionary death of your Son.

Thank you for the divine exchange made possible at the cross, and thank you that I am cleansed and made whole by the blood of the Lord Jesus.

Amen.

DAY 25

He Satisfied the Law

For Christ is the end of the law so that there may be righteousness for everyone who believes.

Romans 10:4

A second way of understanding the work of Jesus on the cross is to understand that as he died, Jesus was fulfilling all the demands and requirements of the Jewish Law, or the Torah.

In his letters to the Roman Christians and the Christians in Galatia, the apostle Paul goes to some length to explain that it was through the Law that the Jewish people were made aware of the nature of sin. Paul suggests that the Law is like a schoolmaster. It explains to its students what is right and what is wrong and instructs them how to live properly and within the confines of God's intentions and desires. In fact, Paul goes slightly further than this. He suggests, in his letter to the Romans, that God will only hold us accountable for that which we know. If he left it there, you would think that those who have never read the Torah would therefore not be held accountable for its instructions. That is true. But Paul also argues that creation itself and a natural sense of what is right and wrong mean that all people everywhere have a basic understanding of right and of wrong, of good and of evil.

So if the Torah lays down a definition of sin and how to live well, why does that have anything to do with the cross and the death of Jesus Christ? For this reason: the Law sets out the expectations and requirements of God for right living, but no person has ever fulfilled those expectations and requirements. We have each chosen our own desires and direction instead of listening to God's instructions and guidance.

The challenge, then, is that we need someone to show us that these laws and expectations are not unrealistic. If someone could do that for us, they would achieve two things at once. Firstly, they would show us that the Torah actually works and obedience to it is possible, albeit difficult. Secondly, they would show us that we are without excuse when it comes to obedience to the Torah, because we have chosen to disregard it because of our nature and our attitude towards God.

Jesus Christ obeyed the Torah to the letter. He fulfilled all of its requirements, not as God but as an observant Jew. He was a faithful human being and he lived in obedience to the Torah. He was disciplined and intentional. If he only did this because of his divine nature, we could rightly say he had more help than we do! However, the Bible is clear that Jesus was a "Second Adam", and that he obeyed and fulfilled the demands of the Torah as a man (1 Corinthians 15:45; Romans 5:12–21). By doing so, he shows us that the Torah is good and that we have wilfully and intentionally failed in our obedience to God. So by satisfying the Law, Jesus becomes the Source of obedience *for* us.

There are two images that will help us here. The first is that the life and ministry of Jesus is like a microcosm of the entire nation of Israel. Where Israel failed, Jesus succeeds. Israel was originally called to live out its relationship with God before the world, so that the world might be blessed through Israel, but Israel failed in this calling. Jesus succeeds where Israel has failed. Jesus *is* faithful Israel, and he shows the world what life can be like when it is lived for God.

Secondly, by fulfilling the requirements of the Torah, Jesus actually completes its purpose, because he is the living Torah. He takes words that are written and demonstrates to the world that they are now lived and witnessed and that their power is available *through* him. There are two interesting little historical facts to mention here. The first is that in the Sermon on the Mount, Jesus makes clear to his listeners that he is the living Torah. They have heard the Torah through Moses, he argues, but now they can see the Torah lived *in* him. The second is that at the time of Jesus' ministry on earth, the Torah was referred to as "the King of the Jews", because it so clearly defined them. When Jesus died, the phrase "The King of the Jews" was placed above his head on the cross. That is because two things were happening – both related to the Torah. The first was that the Torah had been fulfilled and therefore its purpose had changed. The second was that the living Torah, Jesus himself, was hanging beneath the sign.

Prayer

Lord,

I so often convince myself that your demands of me are too high and that you are unrealistic in your expectations of me. Forgive me for defending my selfish behaviour in this way.

Your Law is perfect and it satisfies my soul. Your ways are just and they convert the simple.

Forgive me for my protests. You are not unfair and your expectations are not too high.

Thank you that your Son, Jesus, has shown me what a life lived in obedience to you actually looks like. Thank you that he fulfilled the requirements of the Torah as a man. Thank you that through his obedience, I am confronted with my own selfishness and sin and I am brought to the realization that I have chosen to disobey your commands.

Thank you also that because Jesus has completely obeyed the Torah and fulfilled its requirements, he not only shows me what it looks like to be truly alive but he also offers me his life and power as part of my life. His obedience becomes my obedience. His faithfulness is shared with me.

Thank you that the example of Israel has now been shown to the world. Thank you that we can now see what life is like in your kingdom and as part of your family. Thank you that because of Jesus' faithfulness, the door has been opened for those beyond Israel to become part of your redeemed people. I gladly accept the invitation to be one of the saints.

Thank you that you are now making a new humanity out of those in Israel who call upon your name and those in the Gentile world who call upon your name. Thank you that Jesus' fulfilment of the Torah shows all in Israel that their Law is good, and that his fulfillment of the Law makes it possible for me to know you, love you, serve you, and be transformed by you.

Give me the grace to pay attention to your Word and to walk in your ways because I know that your Word and your Spirit never contradict one another.

Give me grace to discover new depths to the cross.

In Jesus' name,

Amen.

DAY *26*

He Was the Perfect Sacrifice

And he is the atoning sacrifice for our sins, and not for ours only but also for the sins of the whole world.

I John 2:2

In this is love, not that we loved God but that he loved us and sent his Son to be the atoning sacrifice for our sins.

I John 4:10

So we come to the third way in which we can understand the work of Jesus on the cross. Having explored the ideas of penal substitution and of Christ fulfilling the demands of the Torah, we turn our attention to the idea that when Jesus died on the cross, he was offering himself as a sacrifice for our sins. To help explain this idea, we need to explore the beginnings of the story of creation and the early part of the history of the Hebrew people.

In the creation stories recorded in the book of Genesis, we read of the fatal choice of Adam and Eve to ignore God's commands and to rebel against his instructions. In the story recorded in Genesis 3, after they have made this choice to rebel, Adam and Eve become aware of one another's nakedness. The age of innocence has ended. In order to cover their nakedness and their sin, God clothes them in the skins of animals. The implication is clear – to deal with their sin, blood has been shed.

Later in Genesis, the story of Abraham, the father of Israel, is told. Abraham has a son called Isaac. God calls upon Abraham to be willing to sacrifice Isaac. Abraham agrees. As they approach the top of the mountain where Abraham is to kill his son, Isaac asks his father where the sacrificial lamb is, and Abraham replies, "God himself will provide the lamb" (Genesis 22:8).

Later in the story of Israel, the people are held in slavery in Egypt, and God raises up Moses to lead them into freedom and the Promised Land. On the night that Israel is finally released, God passes through Egypt and the firstborn sons of the Egyptians are killed. The Israelites are protected from this terrible fate because they have been commanded, on that night, to kill a young lamb and smear its blood on the doorposts of their homes. The homes that have the mark of the lamb's blood are spared. This is known as the "Passover", because on that night the Angel of the Lord passed over the homes that were marked with the blood of the lamb.

When the Israelites are free from Egypt, they are instructed to set up a tent during their journey in the wilderness, and God instructs them concerning their sacrifices. A lamb or a goat is to be offered as a sacrifice for their sins. This system is repeated later, when Israel builds the Temple in Jerusalem. The lambs that were to be offered were to be perfect, without any blemishes or marks.

When Jesus begins his public ministry, his cousin John the Baptist sees him and describes him as "the Lamb of God who takes away the sin of the world" (John 1:29). Jesus dies on the cross at the time of Passover. The symbolism is rich and significant. He is the pure, spotless, and sinless Lamb of God. His death is the offering of his life on the altar to take away the sins of all those who would call upon his name. The New Testament church picked up this meaning as a very important way of understanding the death of Jesus. Paul, Peter, and John all understood Jesus to be the Lamb of God.

Jesus was the perfect sacrifice because he was *sinless* and *spotless*. But he was also the perfect sacrifice because he was a *willing* sacrifice. The Bible makes it very clear that he came to earth for this very purpose.

He was the *perfect* sacrifice in another way: he was the *full* and *final* sacrifice. His death brought to an end the need for any sacrificial system at all, because all sin – past and present and future – had been dealt with and no other sacrifice would be required.

Christ has paid the great price. He is the Lamb of God who has given his life as a ransom for many. No other ransom will ever be required.

Prayer

Lord,

Thank you for the wonderful thread of Christ's story through the whole Bible.

Thank you that this shows me that the sacrifice of Jesus on the cross was not an accident and it was not an afterthought.

Thank you that all of the sins of the entire world have been dealt with.

Once again, I am left humbled by the example and love of your Son, Jesus. He was like a sheep before his shearers when he was killed. He was meek and gentle and willing. Unlike all the animals sacrificed in the era of the Tabernacle and the Temple, Jesus had a choice, and he chose to lay down his life for me and for the world. Thank you for this willingness.

Thank you for his complete satisfaction of the requirements of the sacrificial system.

Thank you that he came to earth to die for us.

Thank you that his blood is still able to set us free from sin and to release us from our bondage.

Thank you that when the blood of Jesus is applied to my life, it symbolizes my release from death and my entrance into life.

Thank you that you provided yourself, literally, as the Lamb. You did not ask someone else to do it; you came to us, Father, Son, and Holy Spirit, and enabled our salvation.

May I never lose the wonder of the cross and its power.

Amen.

DAY 27

He Overcame Satan

The Son of God was revealed for this purpose, to destroy the works of the devil.

I John 3:8

The fourth way in which we can view the cross is by understanding it as the place where Jesus declared his victory over satan and the powers of hell. On its own, this theory of the atonement would not be sufficient. Indeed, on its own, it creates more questions than it answers. When it is combined with the other theories of the atonement, however, it helps us to see yet another aspect of the way in which the death of Jesus brings us life. This theory is sometimes known as the theory of *Christus Victor* or "Christ the Victor".

In one of the general epistles of John we are told that "the Son of God was revealed for this purpose, to destroy the works of the devil." This idea is also heavily emphasized in the last book of the Bible, which was also written by John – the book of Revelation. In Revelation, satan is cast into a lake of fire and fully and finally defeated forever. The principles behind this way of understanding the death of Jesus are as follows.

Evil exists in the world because of the work of satan. He is the personal originator of sin and the master planner behind all treachery, deceit, and destruction. He comes to the earth to kill, to steal, and to destroy. He was cast out of heaven because of his pride and arrogance and he took one-third of the angelic beings with him, who are now known as demons. They seek to usurp God's authority, destroy God's world, and thwart God's plans. It is satan who tempts the first humans in the creation story, when he comes in the form of a serpent. As God is pronouncing judgment against the serpent, God tells him that he will put enmity between satan and the woman and her offspring. God tells the serpent that the offspring of the woman will bruise the serpent's head and that the serpent will bruise the heel of the woman's offspring. From the earliest days of the church's history, these words have been understood to mean that in the ministry of Jesus, satan was crushed and defeated, but that satan attacked Jesus.

Throughout the history of Israel we see attack after attack on the kingdom of Israel in general and on the tribe of Judah more particularly, and on the line of David most specifically. Reading the story of David's line, one has the impression that there is an attempt to stop something, or perhaps Someone. In the stories of Jesus' life, we see attempts to kill Jesus as a baby, then a direct attempt by satan to tempt him away from his plan at the beginning of his public ministry. Jesus refers to these battles on occasion in his discussions with the disciples, including Simon Peter. As he dies on the cross, Jesus calls out, "It is finished," and then he dies

(John 19:30). This would appear to be the moment of greatest defeat. The apostle Paul, however, sees it very differently. When he writes to the Christians in Colossae, he makes the point that at the moment when all seems lost, and Jesus is dying on the cross, Jesus is actually making a public spectacle of the powers of evil, and satan in particular, because as he dies, Jesus is disarming the powers of darkness (Colossians 2:15).

All this means that in the theory of Christ the Victor, Jesus absorbs all that the powers and forces of evil can throw at him. He carries their insults and their attacks. He absorbs their hatred. As he walks to the cross, Jesus is carrying with him the venom and hatred and injustice and pain of the world, all of which is caused by satan and by evil. As he dies, Jesus is dying *because of this pain and attack.* Jesus' death, in this theory, is God's great "No!" to the sin and the suffering and the destruction caused by satan. However, we know that the cross is not the final word, because when Jesus is resurrected, God is announcing his great "Yes!" to the victory secured by Jesus in the world.

There is no doubt that when Jesus died, he dealt with the power of sin, death, and hell. He dealt with all that satan could throw at him, and he emerged triumphant from the other side of the grave. And because Christ has been victorious over satan, we can be too. His victory secures our victory.

Prayer

Lord,

Thank you for the great victory of your Son over satan on the cross.

Thank you that Jesus came into the world to destroy the works of the evil one.

Thank you that Christianity is not a faith that believes we are locked in a great battle between good and evil where the outcome is uncertain, but instead you have shown us that you have already won the victory over evil. Satan has been defeated. The battle may still be raging, but the outcome has been secured.

I know that there are times in my life when I forget this. I sometimes give satan room in my heart to breed hatred, fear, and distress. I sometimes forget that he was defeated at the cross.

There are times, Lord, when I try to confront evil in my own strength and I quickly fail. I fall and stumble, and it is only then I realize that I have been too proud and tried to resist the devil in my own strength.

Help me to submit myself to you and to remember that as I humble myself and submit myself to you, you give me the strength to resist the devil. Thank you that when I resist the devil, he must flee from me.

I pray for those who have been lulled into thinking that evil is not a real idea. Open their eyes and let them see the battle that rages for their souls. I pray that you will reveal the plan of satan that wants the world to either see him as irrelevant or as equal in power to you. Lord, please help us to realize that your power is greater than satan's, and that when your Son died he stripped the devil of ultimate victory.

I pray for a fresh confidence for your people to confront the works of the enemy in our lives, in our homes, in our churches, and in our nations. I pray for discernment in this battle and for courage to stand in the victory of Jesus Christ.

May all your people become more aware of our freedom in Christ and the power that you have given us in him.

Amen.

DAY *28*

He is the Great Promise-keeper

For in him every one of God's promises is a "Yes." For this reason it is through him that we say the "Amen," to the glory of God.

2 Corinthians 1:20

Jesus never breaks a promise. If he has told you he will do something, he will do it. You can rely on him.

Many people make promises. Some even make promises in the name of Jesus, and then they break those promises. There are many people who will tell you that God has promised you something when God has not promised you that thing. As a result of these "false promises", we can end up thinking that God is somehow unfaithful or unreliable. We must be careful, however, not to blame God for something that he did not do. We must be careful that someone's wrong ideas about God do not leave us with the wrong impression of what God is actually like.

Jesus never promised you an easy life. He did promise that he would never leave you, though. Jesus never promised that he would take away every sickness before you die. He did promise that, for the Christian, death is not the final word, and that all of us would one day be made complete in him. Jesus never promised that society would applaud you and that being a Christian would be something that everyone around you would celebrate, understand, and welcome. He did promise that he would reward you for your faithfulness, though, and that he understands what is happening to you because it also happened to him. Jesus never promised that you would not die for your faith. He did promise that he would welcome you to heaven, though. Jesus never promised that everyone in your family would be converted. He did promise that he loves them and that he would welcome them if they would trust in him.

The Bible contains thousands and thousands of promises that we can cling to because they are given to us as assurances. As Paul makes clear in the verse above, every promise of God relating to salvation and to God's great plan of redemption is fulfilled in Christ. That means that every requirement of the Law for salvation is fulfilled in Jesus' life and ministry. It also means that every promise that is dependent upon the fulfilment of the Law has been fulfilled in Christ. If the cross was the place where God poured out his wrath upon sin and was a divine "No" to sin and its effects upon individuals and the world, then the resurrection is his divine "Yes" to all that can be for those who have been forgiven, cleansed, and accepted.

Every general promise of God is fulfilled and secured by Christ for his people and for the world. That means the promises of protection, grace, life, and hope.

There are other promises in the Bible, though, that we do not like to think about. God has promised to judge the world. He has promised to separate the sheep and the goats at the end of time. All of these promises are also secured in Christ, but we would rather not talk about such things. Perhaps we should. After all, how could God not fulfil his own promises after what his Son has gone through? The cross provides grace, but it also demands a final vindication of the One who died.

One last thought: God still makes promises to individuals and to Christian communities. He still speaks. What he says will never contradict his written Word because the Spirit and the Word never contradict one another. You can be sure of this, however: if God has made you a personal promise, he will fulfil it. Hold on to it if you know for sure it was his promise in the first place. Don't let anyone put you off. Don't let anyone make you give up. Don't let someone who has given up on what God has said to them persuade you to give up on what he has said to you.

Remember – Jesus never breaks a promise. Never. Never. Never.

Prayer

Lord,
I want to stand upon the promises of your Word.
Help me not to fall into the trap of making your Word say something that it does not.

Help me to be robust enough to make sure that what I believe you have said to me is true. Give me friends and brothers and sisters around me who will help me to discern what it is you are saying to me, to our church, and to the nation in which you have placed us.

Then give me the grace to hold on to your promises. Help me to stand upon the promises you have given to your church, to your people, and to me in your Word. Help me also to stand upon the specific and direct promises that you have made to me and to those I know.

Help me not to give up on what you have said because it is delayed in coming or because I have become impatient or tired in waiting. Lord, please grant me faith to keep on trusting in you. Let the gift of faith change my perspective.

Whether I see you or not, remind me you are there. Whether I hear you or not, remind me that you have spoken. Whether your answers are close at hand or far away, help me to seek your face and not just your hand.

Give me the faith to begin praising you now because you never break your promises. Give me childlike joy and expectation once again. Wash away cynicism and apathy by the power of your Holy Spirit.

Help me to remember that every promise you make will be fulfilled – both good promises and promises of holy judgment. Let that spur me on in my service of you and in my passion to see others won to Christ.

Let the promises of your coming kingdom cause me to live well for you, to engage with my world, and to stand as your ambassador and proclaim the gospel fearlessly.

Shine through us, Lord, that the world might see our good deeds and glorify your Father in heaven.

Grant me faith to endure, faith to proclaim, and faith to serve your purposes this day and every day.
Amen.

DAY 29

He Defeated Sin

"He committed no sin, and no deceit was found in his mouth."

When he was abused, he did not return abuse; when he suffered, he did not threaten; but he entrusted himself to the one who judges justly. He himself bore our sins in his body on the cross, so that, free from sins, we might live for righteousness; by his wounds you have been healed. For you were going astray like sheep, but now you have returned to the shepherd and guardian of your souls.

1 Peter 2:22–25 (see also Isaiah 53:4–6)

One of the great puritans of the sixteenth century declared that sin was a brat that no one liked to own. We can behave a little like this, too. We can see wrong happening in the world and throw our hands up in horror, and then quickly point to someone else and suggest that they must have been the cause of that wrong.

We often like to see ourselves as better than we are. Yet here is a fundamentally important question: what good are all the theories of the atonement in the world if they do not liberate us? As long as we hold the ideas of the way the cross works as nothing more than ideas that do not affect us, then the cross has not exercised its power over us or in us. In these next two reflections, I want to move beyond theories of the atonement to think about ways in which Jesus' death on the cross directly deals with the issue of sin in our own lives.

When Jesus died on the cross, he broke the power of sin in our lives and in the lives of all who believe in him. In one sense, this reality is connected to the idea of Christ the Victor that we explored earlier, but what does it mean that Jesus has defeated sin? What are the consequences and implications of his victory for us?

First of all, we should remember that Jesus did not defeat sin by sinning. When he was attacked, he did not attack back. When he was suffering, he did not threaten. Instead he trusted his Father. We can learn from his example. So often, when someone attacks us, our reflex is to attack back. This is the cause of many cycles of violence in families and in nations. Yet Jesus did not defeat violence with violence; he defeated violence with peace. He did not defeat sin with sin; he defeated sin with obedience and faith. He did not defeat hatred with hate; he defeated hatred with love. In this example, he gives us the keys to our own victory over sin. We will overcome sin by reliance on God, not by our own strength and resolve. It is only when we let God live through us that we will experience his victory in us.

Secondly, Jesus' victory over sin means that we do not strive *for* victory but rather we stand *in* victory. *Christ's* victory over sin is now *our* victory over sin. We are not supposed to try harder; we are supposed to trust God more fully. This is an important truth at the heart of Christian faith. Grace not only *saves* us, but grace also *keeps* us. I have met many Christians who talk about gaining victory over sin. I often say to them that they will never manage to gain the victory over sin because Christ has already gained that victory.

Therein lies one of the great mysteries of the cross: Jesus died for us so that we might live. He defeated sin so that we might experience his victory. In order to experience that reality in our own lives, however, we must die to ourselves and let Christ live in us. Up to the point of our conversion, we were in control of our lives. We called the shots. We dictated what would happen next. Of course, there is a sense in which God still gives us choices, but the process of conversion involves us dying to ourselves and living for Christ. It involves us laying aside our old view of the world and the way we used to think, and allowing the new life and new perspective of Christ to live in us and through us. To paraphrase the apostle Paul, when we become Christians we can say that we no longer live, but Christ now lives in us to do his will through us (see Galatians 2:19–20). Christ's victory over sin is ours. Anyone can be a committed Christian; all it takes is the laying down of our lives and the taking up of the cross…

Prayer

Lord,

"I no longer live but Christ lives in me," is such an easy thing to say and such a difficult thing to live. I want to say that

I also live this way, but I know that I do not. I stumble and fall and fail many times.

I thank you that you have fundamentally changed my identity at my conversion. I am no longer controlled by satan and by evil. Christ is now my Captain and my Lord. Yet there are many times when I allow my old worldview to be the dominant voice in my head.

Please help me to move beyond that way of thinking. Remind me that my central identity is now that I am a saint. I am one of your chosen ones. I know I still sin. I know I still falter and fall. I know I still make mistakes, but please help me to remember that as I allow your life to flow through me, your victory will become my victory more and more.

Deliver me from sin. Remind me that you have broken its power in my life and in my thinking. Daily draw me back to the power of your Son, the Lord Jesus, and to the victory that he has secured for me on the cross.

Give me the strength to be shaped by the glorious future that you have set for your children, and do not let me be shaped by my broken and failed past.

Thank you that when I do sin, you have given me your Holy Spirit to convict me, to challenge me, and to change me. Thank you that when I sin, I have your Son, Jesus Christ, defending me, and that his grace and power and forgiveness are constantly at work in my life.

I acknowledge my powerlessness before you, but I also acknowledge your great power in me.

Help me to live in that great power and to continue to be changed from one degree of glory to another.

Amen.

DAY *30*

He Embodies the Gospel for Us

For I handed on to you as of first importance what I in turn had received: that Christ died for our sins in accordance with the scriptures, and that he was buried, and that he was raised on the third day in accordance with the scriptures, and that he appeared to Cephas, then to the twelve.

1 Corinthians 15:3–5

What is the "gospel"?

This is one of the most important questions a Christian can ask. If we mistakenly equate the gospel with being nice people and doing kind things, we will end up creating a better society but not making an eternal difference. Thank God we do not have to guess what the answer to this question is. The apostle Paul sets out the gospel in 1 Corinthians and gives us a clear answer towards the end of his letter. The gospel he describes is centred on Jesus himself, who is the good news! We need to be careful, though, to separate out the mission of Christians and the church and the message of the gospel, because they are not the same thing. If we confuse them, we will end up giving all of our energy and passion to the wrong things and not doing the right things.

The gospel can be summed up like this. Firstly, Jesus Christ died for our sins. We have spent the last few reflections thinking about this. The cross is at the centre of the Christian faith. Jesus came to die, and he came to die *for our sins*. He did not just come to die so that the world would be a better place. His death is not just about creating a nicer and more caring world. His death deals with *sin*. Without this central understanding of the gospel, there is no mission for the church and there is no good news; there is only bad news! Without Jesus' death for our sins, we are left with a self-help message that tells us to try harder, do more, pray more, put a bit more effort in. Without the death of Jesus for our sins as the heartbeat of Christianity, we are left with our own strength and trying to change the world out of our own reserves – and that will not last!

Secondly, the gospel tells us that Jesus was actually buried. Why is that important? It is important because it means that Jesus tasted and experienced death itself for us. On the cross he defeated our great enemy – sin. In the grave he overcame our great fear – death. Death itself has been swallowed up by the death of Jesus.

Thirdly, the gospel tells us that Jesus was resurrected. He did not stay dead! Having borne our sin and died our death, he then broke the chains of sin and burst out of the prison of death in glorious life to declare that this really is *Good News!*

How do we know these three fundamental truths of the gospel? For two reasons: the first and most important is that these things happened *in accordance with the Scriptures.* If we want to know what the gospel is, we allow the Scriptures to tell us. Remember, Jesus came to fulfil the Scriptures, not to destroy them. The second reason we know these fundamentals are true is because of the witnesses to the events in the life of Jesus that we have outlined. Cephas (Peter) and the twelve saw Jesus die. They were alive when he was buried, and the resurrected Jesus met with them and talked with them.

It is this good news that has changed the world. And what is our response to this good news as Christians? Firstly, we give ourselves to proclaiming it in our own words. We are clear about the core of the gospel. Our primary response to the gospel is to believe it, to declare it, and to make disciples who believe it too. Secondly, we allow the gospel and the reality of the living Jesus to shape the way we engage with the world. We seek to engage in the mission of the church – which is the making of disciples who themselves make disciples. And we cannot be disciples without making a difference in the world. To truly believe this gospel is to give ourselves in service to the least, the last, and the lost, and to see the world transformed by the power of the resurrected Jesus.

Prayer

Lord,
Thank you for the simplicity and the power of the gospel.
Thank you that Jesus died for our sins according to the Scriptures.
Thank you that he was buried and that he rose on the third day according to the Scriptures.

Thank you that he appeared to the apostles and many others.
May this life-changing message of Christ's power continually change me and inspire me. May I always remember that Jesus died for my sins and that he conquered sin on the cross and death in the tomb, and that he brought new life and a new creation in his resurrection.
May this life-changing, world-changing, earth-transforming message be captured again by your church, and may we give ourselves to your purposes with renewed passion, vision, and faith.
Help us to make disciples who make disciples…
Help us to give ourselves to this primary task with all we have.
Help us to be disciples who understand how to make a difference.
Let your church shine for you in the world, now and forever.
Let us be found among the least, the last, and the lost.
Let us declare the hope and message of the gospel in all that we do and all that we are, and let that start in my life, my family, my local church, my community, and my world.
Amen.

DAY *31*

He Descended to the Dead

This man went to Pilate and asked for the body of Jesus. Then he took it down, wrapped it in a linen cloth, and laid it in a rock-hewn tomb where no one had ever been laid.

Luke 23:52–53

Therefore it is said,

"When he ascended on high he made captivity itself a captive; he gave gifts to his people."

(When it says, "He ascended," what does it mean but that he had also descended into the lower parts of the earth? He who descended is the same one who ascended far above all the heavens, so that he might fill all things.)

Ephesians 4:8–10

For Christ also died for sins once for all, the just for the unjust, so that He might bring us to God, having been put to death in the flesh, but made alive in the spirit; in which also He went and made proclamation to the spirits now in prison, who once were disobedient, when the patience of God kept waiting in the days of Noah, during the construction of the ark, in which a few, that is, eight persons, were brought safely through the water.

1 Peter 3:18–20 (NASB)

We have explored why Jesus died and what he was doing for us, but what happened to him when he died? There have always been those who believed that he did not really die. Even in the early days of Christianity, there were some who believed that Jesus merely fainted or swooned. The Gospels themselves indicate that the Roman and Jewish authorities tried to spread this rumour.

Through the history of the church there have been men and women who have tried to change this part of the life of Jesus. I have spoken to many people who engage in this conversation as if we are the first generation to struggle with the idea that Jesus died. We are not the first to wrestle with the idea. It isn't exactly news that dead people are supposed to stay dead, is it? And if they don't stay dead (which we will come to later) then they must not have been dead in the first place, right? Wrong.

The New Testament makes the unequivocal claim that Jesus actually died. The details in the story of the crucifixion, particularly around the last moments of Jesus' life, when water and blood flowed from his side when it was pierced, together with the details of the removal of his body and his burial, all tell us that Jesus died. He did not swoon. He was not faking death. He did not simply pass out. He died.

We know what happened to his physical body when he died – it was taken to an unused tomb and laid to rest, but what happened to his spirit or his soul? The Bible doesn't actually give us a definitive answer. One view is that he went to Hades, the place of the dead, and proclaimed truth to those who were there. Some people think his audience was all those who had died before the cross, and others think it was those who died in the flood of Noah. Others believe that when Jesus died he descended to "Abraham's bosom" (a place where the Jews believed the righteous awaited judgment), where he proclaimed the truth and led to heaven those who had been waiting there.

Whatever Jesus did when he was dead, there are a few obvious implications. Firstly, his death impacted all of history, including all those who had died before his own crucifixion. Secondly, his death was genuine and real in every human sense of the word. Thirdly, the fact that he returned means that he defeated death. Death did not defeat Jesus – and we will come to that wonderful truth in our next reflection.

Prayer

Lord Jesus,
Thank you that you descended to the dead.
Thank you that your death was not a fake or a pretence.
Thank you that all of history and all of time is impacted by your descent to the dead.
Thank you that you announced the truth to those who were there when you descended to the dead.

Thank you that your power goes beyond our understanding and that there are many aspects of your ministry and life that we do not understand.

Thank you that your victory was complete and that no one has missed the opportunity of experiencing your grace and your mercy.

Thank you that death did not defeat you – you defeated it.

And thank you that the only way we can understand that is by one day meeting you face to face, when you shall make all things clear.

Help us to live beyond the fear of death because you have plundered it.

Amen.

DAY *32*

He Defeated Death by Resurrection

Early on Sunday morning, while it was still dark, Mary Magdalene cane to the tomb and found that the stone had been rolled away from the entrance. She ran and found Simon Peter and the other disciple, the one whom Jesus loved. She said, "They have taken the Lord's body out of the tomb, and we don't know where they have put him!"… Mary was standing outside the tomb crying, and as she wept, she stooped and looked in. She saw two white-robed angels, one sitting at the head and the other at the foot of the place where the body of Jesus had been lying. "Dear woman, why are you crying?" the angels asked her.

"Because they have taken away my Lord," she replied, "and I don't know where they have put him."

She turned to leave and saw someone standing there. It was Jesus but she didn't recognize him.

John 20:1–2, 11–14 (NLT)

Christ has been raised from the dead, the first fruits of those who have died. For since death came through a human being, the resurrection of the dead has also come through a human being; for as all die in Adam, so all will be made alive in Christ … The last enemy to be destroyed is death …

"Death has been swallowed up in victory."

"Where, O death, is your victory?

Where, O death, is your sting?"

The sting of death is sin, and the power of sin is the law. But thanks be to God, who gives us the victory through our Lord Jesus Christ.

1 Corinthians 15:20–22, 26, 54–57 (see also Isaiah 25:8; Hosea 13:14)

Every Easter Sunday, our church is filled with light and colour. It is a massive contrast to the starkness of Good Friday. Why do we go to such trouble? For the simple reason that, as we have seen earlier, if the cross and the death of Jesus are God's great "No!" to sin and death, then the resurrection is God's great "Yes!" to new life and to hope.

I think every church should encourage every Christian to light all their lights and to throw a great party on Easter Sunday. We are Easter People! Jesus may have died, but he did not stay dead. Three days after he was placed in a tomb, he rose from the dead. And as he rose, a new creation began. Creation began in a garden in Eden and ends in a garden city in the book of Revelation. The New Creation begins in a garden just outside Jerusalem where

Mary encounters Jesus as the gardener! The imagery is incredibly powerful, and the message is clear. This is the moment that the risen, conquering, victorious Jesus begins his ascent to his Father. Having descended to the very depths of creation – death itself – he is now alive again and on his way to the highest point of creation, the right hand of his Father in heaven.

Nothing will ever be the same again. The disciples will have their lives turned inside out, and over the next forty or fifty years the world will be turned upside down. Billions of people since that moment have encountered the living, breathing, death-defeating Jesus. The same Jesus who was raised from the dead now lives in every person who has called upon his name. He is present in every group of people who gather to worship him, whether that be under a tree in Asia or Africa, in a cathedral in Rome, or in your church building in your town or city.

Jesus is alive and well. He is changing lives and ushering in his reign and rule, and we need never, ever fear death, sin, or the devil again. Now that is worth celebrating! So crack open the champagne and have a party – because the victory is secure and new creation has begun! Hallelujah!

But how can Jesus be in two places at once? Read on, dear friend, read on!

Prayer

Lord,

I was not made for death, so when I face it I still feel some level of anxiety and concern.

Thank you that when your Son was raised from the dead, he shattered the darkness. The shadows of death are present but the reality is changed forever for those who trust in him.

I know that I still allow it to affect me, and I ask you to shake away its grip from my thinking and my attitude. Help me to remember that the resurrection of Jesus means that death is dealt with.

Help me to remember that the resurrection of Jesus means that I will be reunited with those who have gone to be with you already.

Help me to remember that because Jesus has been resurrected, I will be too. He is the firstborn from among the dead, but his resurrection is the guarantee of my resurrection and the resurrection of all who have died in Christ.

Thank you that the resurrection is like spring for the whole earth, that the New Creation is bursting out throughout the universe.

Help me to remember the hope that resurrection brings.

I pray for those who have lost loved ones – may they be given great hope and comfort from the truth of your Son's victory over death.

And may his victory enable me to face death without fear or anxiety – both my own death and the deaths of those whom I know and love.

Yours the glory and yours the victory, now and for evermore.

Amen.

DAY *33*

He Ascended to Heaven

"But you will receive power when the Holy Spirit has come upon you; and you will be my witnesses in Jerusalem, in all Judea and Samaria, and to the ends of the earth." When he had said this, as they were watching, he was lifted up, and a cloud took him out of their sight. While he was going and they were gazing up toward heaven, suddenly two men in white robes stood by them. They said, "Men of Galilee, why do you stand looking up toward heaven?"

Acts 1:8–11

The Lord Jesus Christ's ascension to heaven is only right and proper.

Having been born on the earth, having lived and walked among us, and having been confined by time and space and history, Jesus' earthly mission is complete and he is taken back to heaven. His ascension actually begins with his resurrection, but he spends forty days instructing his disciples about his kingdom before he continues his journey home to be with his Father.

The ascension is often overlooked in nonconformist churches like mine. Perhaps that is because it is on a Thursday. I suspect that many Christians don't really see it as particularly important. For many it is better to think about the cross, the resurrection, Pentecost, and his second coming. Yet the ascension of Jesus is vital if we are to understand the rest of his ministry.

Firstly, the ascension creates a bridge between Jesus' earthly incarnate ministry and his heavenly incarnate ministry. Note that Jesus is still human. He has now received his resurrection body, and that will remain with him forever. The ascension links the earthly ministry of Jesus, including his death and resurrection, to his ongoing intercessory ministry in heaven.

Secondly, his ascension is the beginning of Jesus' vindication. This will not be complete until he finally returns to rule and reign upon the earth. In his ascension, however, the apostles witness Jesus' departure from the earth. They see him leave the surface of earth. This is yet another confirmation to them that Jesus is who he claimed to be, and it must have filled them with awe and confidence.

Thirdly, his ascension tells us something about his return, because the promise given to the witnesses is that Jesus would come back.

Fourthly, the ascension of Jesus means that a new phase of his ministry can now begin. As we will see in the next reflection, that new phase of ministry continues to link Jesus to us here on the earth in a number of ways. The disciples needed to know that although he was going away, he was not leaving them. The words that he spoke to them just before he ascended gave them that assurance.

Lastly, Jesus' ascension opens the way for the coming of the Holy Spirit, because as long as Jesus was on the earth in physical form – even in his resurrected physical form – he could only be in one place at any one time. For the ministry of the gospel and the message of the cross to spread around the world, Jesus needed a new body on the earth with his resurrected body elsewhere. That new body on earth would be his Bride, the church, which would be birthed just a few days after his ascension.

We must never forget that Jesus has ascended. To do so is to allow ourselves to think that he is not here, or that he has forgotten us. Neither of those things is true at all. He has ascended, but he has done so for specific purposes and to achieve specific things, one of which is to pray for us.

Prayer

Lord Jesus,
Remind me of the power and the purpose of your ascension.
When I think you have left me or forgotten about me, remind me that you have not.
Thank you that you are now free to be present in the life of every believer everywhere.
Thank you that you are no longer confined by time, space, or geography.
Thank you that the time of your curtailment has ended.
Thank you that you continue to carry me on your heart.
Thank you that you have not abandoned your world or deserted your church.

Strengthen your people, Lord, wherever they are and whatever they face.

Remind us that your ascension also signals the nature of your return, and help us to live with expectation, hope, and faith strong in our hearts.

Amen.

DAY *34*

He is by His Father's Side

"Look," he said, "I see the heavens opened and the Son of Man standing at the right hand of God!"

Acts 7:56

But God, who is rich in mercy, out of the great love with which he loved us even when we were dead through our trespasses, made us alive together with Christ – by grace you have been saved – and raised us up with him and seated us with him in the heavenly places in Christ Jesus, so that in the ages to come he might show the immeasurable riches of his grace in kindness toward us in Christ Jesus.

Ephesians 2:4–7

So if you have been raised with Christ, seek the things that are above, where Christ is, seated at the right hand of God.

Colossians 3:1

Furthermore, the former priests were many in number, because they were prevented by death from continuing in office; but he holds his priesthood permanently, because he continues forever. Consequently he is able for all time to save those who approach God through him, since he always lives to make intercession for them.

Hebrews 7:23–25

So what exactly is Jesus doing now? Just because we cannot see him, it does not mean that he cannot see us, or that he has forgotten us.

Firstly, Jesus is praying for us. Jesus now stands before his Father and intercedes for us. This should fill us with great hope and confidence. Do you think Jesus ever prays outside of his Father's will? Do you think he is ever confused about what to ask his Father to do? Of course not. He is the perfect intercessor, because he is also the perfect mediator. In fact, the Bible makes it clear that we do not need any other mediator in heaven. There is no one else in heaven who could represent us better.

Secondly, there is no one in heaven who is closer to God the Father than God the Son. Jesus Christ is at the very right hand of God. He is not at a distance from God. He does not need to wait in line. He has the Father's ear and he is in the Father's presence and he has the Father's attention. The wonderful thing is that in that very place he prays and intercedes for us.

Thirdly, he has lifted us to this wonderful place of intimacy with him. Although we are on earth, we, too, as his children, can enter the very throne room of God with great confidence and boldness. There is no bar to our communion with Almighty God.

Jesus, our Saviour, has opened the way for us to have continual and open communion with his Father.

Lastly, the priesthood of Jesus is established permanently and securely. He has tasted death and defeated it. He has completed his earthly ministry and is now able to stand eternally before the presence of his Father. He may stand to welcome us into his presence, as he did with Stephen, but his normal position is one of regency and reign, seated at the right hand of his Father. It is a place of authority, power, and dominion, and the world sits at his feet as he upholds it with his every word.

Prayer

Lord Jesus,
Thank you that you are at the very right hand of your Father.
Thank you that in your heavenly ministry you are praying and interceding for all your people.
Thank you that you lift us into the very presence of your Father despite the earthly challenges and limitations that we sometimes feel.
Thank you that you are the audience before whom we now live our lives.
Help me to fix my eyes on you, the One who is the Pioneer and the Perfector, the Author and the Finisher of my faith.
Thank you that you always pray the perfect prayer for me.
Thank you that you never forget me.
I pray for all those who feel forgotten around the world, and particularly for those who think you have forgotten them. Turn their attention to you again. Strengthen your church and protect your people.

May we live in the light of the assurance that you are watching us, ready to welcome us, and praying for us now.
We give you praise and glory.
Amen.

DAY 35

He is the Baptizer in the Holy Spirit

"And afterward,
I will pour out my Spirit on all people.
Your sons and daughters will prophesy,
your old men will dream dreams,
your young men will see visions."

Joel 2:28 (NIV)

And I will give you a new heart, and I will put a new spirit in you. I will take out your stony, stubborn heart and give you a tender, responsive heart.

Ezekiel 36:26 (NLT)

"'He on whom you see the Spirit descend and remain is the one who baptizes with the Holy Spirit.' And I myself have seen and have testified that this is the Son of God."

John 1:33–34

"Do not leave Jerusalem until the Father sends you the gift he promised, as I told you before. John baptized with water, but in just a few days you will be baptized with the Holy Spirit."

Acts 1:4–5 (NLT)

When John the Baptist saw Jesus coming to be baptized in the River Jordan, John declared that Jesus was the one who would baptize people with the Holy Spirit. This baptism first took place on the Day of Pentecost, which is recorded in Acts 2, but Jesus himself promised that he would do this in Acts 1 and in the Gospel of John.

What does it mean to be baptized in the Holy Spirit, and why is it important that Jesus is the one who baptizes us?

To understand the baptism of the Holy Spirit and its significance, we have to journey all the way back to the Old Testament. The celebration of Pentecost was originally a harvest festival for the Jews, when they remembered the goodness and faithfulness of God in providing them with all that they needed for life. It was sometimes called the Day of Firstfruits or the Feast of Weeks. It was a time of great joy and celebration as the Jews remembered the provision and the grace and the abundance of God. It is fitting, then, that God would choose to pour out his Holy Spirit during this festival.

Throughout the history of Israel, God promised that a time would come when he would place his Spirit inside the lives of those who believed in him and trusted in him. They would not only have an external Torah; they would have the living presence of God himself within them to guide them. This is what happened on the day of Pentecost.

Jesus poured out the Holy Spirit from heaven, and the Holy Spirit took up residence in the lives of every single believer who was present in the upper room in Jerusalem where they were meeting. The evidence of his presence was that they spoke in languages they had not learned, and they could see fire resting upon one another. They also heard a mighty wind blowing through the room. Wind and fire are symbols of the Holy Spirit in the Bible, as are many others such as oil, fire, a dove and breath.

The power of the Holy Spirit had an immediate impact. The disciples were given great boldness to bear witness to Jesus and who he was, and many people were converted in Jerusalem that day. In fact, 3,000 people were converted, which is exactly the same number as those who died on the day Moses left Mount Sinai in the book of Exodus (Exodus 32:25–29 – note verse 28). This is yet another evidence that the Spirit was bringing the presence of Jesus, the Living Torah, into his people.

The reason that Jesus is the Baptizer is that the Holy Spirit is another part of the Godhead. He is exactly like Jesus. He makes Jesus real in the lives of Christians. He convicts us of sin, he guides us in truth, and he defends us before the world. He gives us gifts for mission and service. He produces fruit so that we behave like Jesus. He enables us to point people to Jesus and he reminds us that we are God's children, and he defends us from the attacks and the criticisms of the devil. He is promised to every believer, and we need him to fill us as often as we need to breathe. Without him, we can do nothing.

Prayer

Lord Jesus,
I need your Spirit to fill me with every single breath.
Without you, I can achieve nothing of worth or value or purpose.
Only you can fill me with your Holy Spirit, so I pray that you will fill me afresh.
Please give me the power to live for you, and if needs be, the power to die for you.
Please give me the courage to speak for you.
Please give me the boldness to declare you.
Please give me the gifts that I require to fulfil my calling in you.
Please grow the fruit of the Spirit in me, that others might see Jesus in my life.
Please guide me by your Spirit.
Please give me a deeper assurance of my adoption into your family, and help me to daily live in the new intimacy and identity that you have given me as your child.
Please help me to listen to your Holy Spirit and to follow where he might lead me.
Please illuminate your Word by the power of your Holy Spirit, and help me to fall deeper in love with Jesus.
Please create new intimacy in my worship and prayer life by the power of the Holy Spirit.
Please strengthen my mission and witness for you by the power of the Holy Spirit.
Come and meet with me now, I pray.
Amen.

DAY 36

He is All We Long for

His divine power has given us everything needed for life and godliness, through the knowledge of him who called us by his own glory and goodness. Thus he has given us, through these things, his precious and very great promises, so that through them you may escape from the corruption that is in the world because of lust, and may become participants of the divine nature.

2 Peter 1:3–4

Many years ago, when I was at Bible College, I was asked to preach in the corporate devotions of the community. I chose this text to preach on. I believed it then, and I believe it still. At the time, there was a great deal of spiritual renewal taking place around the world, and I was deeply thankful to God for what he was doing. Lives were being changed and people were discovering a new depth of intimacy with God and a new vibrancy in their spirituality. It was wonderful. At the same time, though, there was a wave of spirituality sweeping across the church in North America and Europe that was suggesting that what God had done in Jesus wasn't enough. The argument was that we needed "more of God". Having Christ as our Saviour, our Redeemer, our Baptizer, and our Sustainer wasn't enough. That's just not true.

I understand what people mean when they say, "I need more of you, Lord!" They are saying they want a deeper experience of the reality of God in their lives. They want to walk more closely with him. They want to see him more clearly. They want to be more sensitive to his leading. They want to be more submitted to his will and more open to his Spirit's guidance and leading and enabling. I say a hearty, full-blooded "Amen!" to all of that. Yet the reality is that we are actually saying, "Lord, have more of me," not, "Lord, give me more of you!"

While for many the argument may be pedantic, I think it is important. There are many in the church who are constantly seeking a new high. Their confidence in God is only as good as the last experience. That is not only wrong biblically; it is dangerous. Our faith impacts our wills, our emotions, our intellects, and our actions and attitudes. It should impact every area of our lives. Christian faith *must* have an impact on our emotions. If it does not, then there is a defect in our understanding of our faith.

There is a world of difference, however, between a faith that impacts our emotions and a faith that is driven by our emotions. While the first is helpful and right, the second is detrimental to our spiritual lives, and it is wrong. We must be very careful not to allow ourselves to fall into the trap of thinking that what Christ has done for us is not enough. The idea that we somehow need

God to do "more" undermines what he has already done for us in Christ.

There are two opposite dangers that we must avoid. The first is the notion that we need to move beyond Jesus. The second is that we somehow just need to offer an intellectual assent to what Christ has done and we will have all we need. These are dangerous arguments at opposite ends of a spectrum. The end that is driven by always needing more will lead to a loss of assurance and a deep sense of spiritual confusion, while the end that is driven by dry intellectual assent leads to spiritual lifelessness and christianized presumption and apathy.

What we need is a daily apprehension of all that Christ has given us, is giving us, and will give us. By using the term "apprehension" I do not only mean understanding; I use it to mean a fully orbed act of taking hold of all that Christ has done for us, is doing, and will do. This involves the will, the intellect, the emotions, and the heart. We recognize that Christ has done it all, that the Spirit is given to us so that we can lay hold of all that Jesus has done for us, become what Jesus has enabled us to be, and grow ever closer to the God who has drawn close to us. In effect, we grow in our experience of our salvation. We become what he has already made us. We grow closer to the One who is already close to us. We experience the One who is already indwelling us. We are drawn into the embrace of the One who is already embracing us.

Christ is all we need, and he is enough! His grace, mercy, power, and love are made real to us by the power of the Holy Spirit. He needs more of us, which is what we mean when we say, "We need more of you, Lord!"

Prayer

Lord,

I do not want to fall into the trap of being apathetic, cynical, cold, and lifeless. Nor do I want to fall into the error of turning my relationship with you into some kind of spiritual roller coaster where I am constantly seeking another high. Please forgive me when either of these attitudes has gripped my heart or my head.

Help me to become more and more controlled, led, shaped, and centred around the work you have done in my life through the death, life, and resurrection of your Son, the Lord Jesus. Help me to step out of the centre of my own life and to allow you to be at the centre of my thinking, my emotions, my longings, and my decisions.

Thank you that there is so much more of you for me to know. I understand so little of who you are and what you have done for me. Help me to step out of the shallows of my spirituality and into the depths of what you have given me in your Son.

Take me further in revelation, Lord. Show me what you have secured for me in your Son. Show me the depth of the assurance of my faith. Let a passion and desire for you become so strong in my heart that it will drive out selfishness, bitterness, and shallowness. Let my life be thrown at your feet.

Lord, let me grasp the depth and height and breadth of my salvation. Please let me see the glory and wonder of your plans for the world and for your people. Let me see Jesus more clearly. Let me understand more profoundly what he has done for those who love him. Deliver me from a small and petty spirituality.

Lord, help me never to become cynical of what you are doing in the world. Let me pray for those who are encountering you in fresh and new ways instead of standing in judgment over them.

Do whatever you want to do in my life, Lord. Do whatever you want to do in the lives of those who love you. Help me to be open to the leading of your Spirit and ready to follow the wind of your guidance.

Thank you for everything you have given us in Christ. Thank you that he has secured everything for us. Thank you that you reveal what he has done for us, what he is doing for us, and what he will do for us through your Word and by your Spirit.

Give me the grace, the courage, and the conviction to live out the full salvation you have secured for me both fearlessly and faithfully. Let me become all you have already made me to be. Let me lay hold of that for which you have already laid hold of me. Let me be what you have made me to be.

Amen.

DAY 37

He is the Returning King

"Jesus has been taken from you into heaven, but someday he will return from heaven in the same way you saw him go."

Acts 1:11 (NLT)

But we do not want you to be uninformed, brothers, about those who are asleep, that you may not grieve as others do who have no hope. For since we believe that Jesus died and rose again, even so, through Jesus, God will bring with him those who have fallen asleep. For this we declare to you by a word from the Lord, that we who are alive, who are left until the coming of the Lord, will not precede those who have fallen asleep. For the Lord himself will descend from heaven with a cry of command, with the voice of an archangel, and with the sound of the trumpet of God. And the dead in Christ will rise first. Then we who are alive, who are left, will be caught up together with them in the clouds to meet the Lord in the air, and so we will always be with the Lord. Therefore encourage one another with these words.

1 Thessalonians 4:13–18 (ESV)

"See, I am coming soon! Blessed is the one who keeps the words of the prophecy of this book." ...

The one who testifies to these things says, "Surely I am coming soon."

Amen. Come, Lord Jesus!

Revelation 22:7, 20

We have almost reached the end of our little book of reflections on the person of the Lord Jesus Christ. We began this journey by thinking about the fact that all the books in the entire world could not describe him. I have tried to tease out some of the truths about his character and nature and ministry from around a hundred verses in the Bible. There are approximately 31,173 verses in the Bible and around 1,189 chapters. It will not come as a surprise, therefore, that I have only skimmed the surface.

I trust you have enjoyed the journey. Soon I hope to write a companion volume to this one in which I will look at the character of Jesus as seen through each of the sixty-six books of the Bible. This will give me the chance to explore his life with you a little more. For now, however, I want to turn my attention to the promised return of King Jesus.

The Bible makes it clear that Jesus Christ will not stay in heaven, but instead he will return to the earth. There is a great deal of discussion about when he will return, how he will return, and what will happen to the church when he returns.

These subjects cause great debate and, sadly, great dissension in the church.

I want to highlight just a few thoughts about the reality of King Jesus' return to planet earth.

Firstly, he will return as the great and glorious King that he has always been. This is only fitting, since it will be the full and final vindication of his life and ministry.

Secondly, he will return to reign. The Bible makes it very clear that he will finally consummate his kingdom when he returns. There will be no more sorrow or pain or suffering, and all things will be made new.

Thirdly, when he returns, those who have died in Christ and those who are alive will be reunited. That will be a wonderful moment in time and history.

Fourthly, his return will be announced with the voice of the archangel and with the trumpet call of God. This will be the greatest moment that history has ever seen.

Fifthly, he will return to the air above Jerusalem, and then he will bring those who have been caught up to be with him to the earth.

Christians are called to encourage one another with these truths and to spur one another on to live in the light of Christ's return. There simply are no words to describe this event and its significance in the history of the world or as the consummation of the purposes of God. The Jesus who was born in a stable to a poor mother and father will return as the great and glorious and manifestly attested Son of God. It will be a day of great encouragement to many, but a day of great fear to others.

Prayer

Lord Jesus,
It seems only right that when you return you will do so in great glory and amid great celebration and joy.
Thank you that you will come for your Bride, the church.
Please help us to live with your return in view.
Help us to be ready.
Help us to be expectant.
Help us to be hopeful.
Forgive us when we forget that you will return.
Forgive me when I live my life as if you are an irrelevance.
Forgive us when we make your return a subject of argument, or when we ignore it because we do not understand all of the aspects of your arrival.
Please help us to encourage one another and to spur one another on to good works in the light of your promised return. When we find life hard, when we are opposed, when we are persecuted for our faith, remind us that you see what is happening and you have not forgotten us. Please cause faith to rise in our hearts at such moments and courage to grow.
Thank you that when you return, you will establish your kingdom and that pain and suffering will be no more.
Thank you that when you return, we will be reunited with those who have died in Christ and gone before us.
May we live for your glory and your fame.
We look to you and your return, King Jesus.
Amen.

DAY *38*

He is Our First and Last Word

Then God said, "Let there be light"; and there was light.

Genesis 1:3

In the beginning was the Word, and the Word was with God, and the Word was God.

John 1:1

"I am the Alpha and the Omega, the first and the last, the beginning and the end."

Revelation 22:13

There can be an unsettling tendency for many Christians to try to go beyond the gospel. We can end up like the Galatian followers of Jesus. Paul had to write to them to ask them what had happened to them. Having been converted by grace, they had reverted to legalism and to formalism. They thought they had gone beyond the gospel.

The truth is that we never go beyond the gospel. How can we? It is in Jesus we see the full purposes and plans of God. He is our first and our last word, and he is every word in between.

He is the first word because he was there at the very beginning, present in creation itself. He is the first word because he is the perfect word. In him, we see exactly what God is like. He is the first word because he takes the initiative and comes to us. It was while we were still sinners that he died for us. He loved us first. We love him as a response to his love. He came looking for us; we did not go looking for him. He opened our hearts to his love; we did not open them ourselves. He is the first word.

He is also the last word. He is the last word because nothing needs to be added to what he has done. Nothing can make the cross more powerful than it already is. Jesus does not just tell us the way of salvation; Jesus *is* the way of salvation. He is the last word because he is the fulfilling word. The requirements of the Law are met in him. The sacrifices required are made by him. Prophecy finds its fulfilment in him. He is the last word because he is the final word. His cry on the cross, "Finished", is the seal of security on the affidavit of our faith. He is the last word because he alone has done it. He has plundered hell, and he alone. He has defeated sin, and he alone. He has broken the bars that incarcerated us, and he has pushed open the prison doors. The chains that he breaks cannot become fetters once again. He is the last word because all things are complete. The task has been completed. The assignment has been finished. He is the last word because he is the only word. That is why Peter could cry out to the early church that there was no other name given among people by which they could be saved.

He is the first and the last word because he has told us he is. He declared himself to be the Way, the Truth, and the Life.

There is no other way because no other way is needed. You cannot improve upon perfection. One day Perfection will return to the earth in physical form, and at that moment all that points towards him will bow before him. He is our first and final word because he is the answer to all of our questions about life and death and heaven and hell and hope and grace and love and beauty and meaning.

Jesus is not simply a picture or a metaphor or an idea; he is the grace of God made manifest to us. He is the forgiveness of God made available to us. He is not just the Sustainer of creation; he is the Sustainer of re-creation. He has made, is making, and will make all things new. He is the first and the last word because beyond him there is nothing to say.

Do you know him? Do you really know him? I do not ask whether you know *about* him. I ask you, do you know him?

Prayer

Lord,

You have come to us in your Son in a complete, beautiful way. There is nothing we can add to him. There are no words to express to you what we feel as we reflect upon his matchless beauty and grace.

Thank you that to know him is to know life eternal. Thank you that he alone holds the words of eternal life. Thank you that he has perfectly, faithfully, and fully revealed you to us. Thank you that we do not need to try and fill in the blanks.

Yet, Lord, we see you dimly at times. We know that this is because we walk by faith and not by sight. We know that we understand less than we would like to, but we acknowledge that the lack lies in us and not in you. The Lord Jesus has faithfully and fully shown us who you are, but we know we do not always look at him properly.

Forgive us for the times we look at him fleetingly, and by so doing we miss the opportunity of seeing the depths of his beauty.

Forgive us for the times we look at him through the lens of our pain or our suffering or our circumstances, and by so doing we see him wrongly.

Forgive us when we look at him through the lens of the traditions or our religion, and we try to make him something that he is not by chaining him to wrong customs or habits or ideas. Forgive us when we try to make him a Protestant or a Roman Catholic or an Orthodox or a Baptist or an Anglican or a Pentecostal.

Forgive us when we look at him through the lens of our culture and we try to make him fit our culture's definition of goodness or love.

Forgive us when we try to make Jesus look like us instead of seeking to let you make us look like Jesus.

He is the first and the last word. He is the author and the finisher of our faith. He is all that we need and all that we long to be. He is what our hearts yearn for. O God of grace and love and mercy, set a flame of love ablaze in our hearts that will consume our selfishness and pride and sin and will burn ever more brightly for him. Cause us to become ever more captured by the name of Jesus.

We worship you.

Amen.

DAY 39

He is Our Groom and We are His Bride

Then I heard what seemed to be the voice of a great multitude, like the sound of many waters and like the sound of mighty thunderpeals, crying out,

"Hallelujah!
For the Lord our God
the Almighty reigns.
Let us rejoice and exult
and give him the glory,
for the marriage of the Lamb has come,
and his bride has made herself ready;
to her it has been granted to be clothed
with fine linen, bright and pure" –
for the fine linen is the righteous deeds of the saints.

Revelation 19:6–8

There is no more wonderful picture of Jesus than the picture of a groom waiting for his bride.

A groom has wooed his bride. He has tended to her. He has loved her. He has spent time with her and she with him. He has learned some of the quirky ways that his bride has and he loves her still. He has committed himself to her. He has prepared himself for intimacy with her. He has ensured that the wedding is ready. He has fallen more and more in love with her. He has pursued her. He has betrothed himself to her. He has dressed for her.

Jesus, our Groom, awaits us. This is not a relationship of transaction. This is not a business deal, although he has bought us with his blood. Our relationship with him is not simply that of lord and servant, although it is surely that. Our relationship with him is not one of teacher and pupil, although this is also true. He is not simply our Saviour, our Redeemer, our Restorer, our Friend, and our Brother; he is also our Groom. What a beautiful picture.

And how do we respond as his bride? Are we ready for the great wedding? Have we adorned ourselves with the jewels of good works and faith and faithfulness that he has given us? Have we readied ourselves for our ever-deeper union with him? Are we still in love with him? Does he cause our hearts to miss a beat? Does his name make us catch our breath? When we think of him do we smile in anticipation? Is our first thought how we might make him happy? Do we awake each morning with his name on our lips and his love in our hearts? When we go to bed at night, do we want our day to have pleased him? Have we enjoyed our courtship? Have we spent moments of intimacy together? Have we shared our dreams and longings with him? Have we allowed ourselves to be vulnerable before him? Have we shared the secrets of our hearts with him?

The Lord Jesus is all that the words of this little book have sought to reveal, but he is so much more. We cannot capture the depth of the love he has shown us – but the idea of a groom awaiting his bride goes some of the way. We are, together, his bride. He will come for us. He will announce the wedding banquet and we will be united with him forever – a unity that will never be broken and will never be false.

With such wonderful beauty in this metaphor I find myself reticent to issue a word of caution, but I feel I must. To those of us who are pastors, leaders, elders, and the like in the bride of Christ – the church – there is a word of warning. We would not sleep with another man's wife so we must be careful not to assume the position or function of the groom. The church is not our bride. We must always remember that we are part of the bride; we are *never* the groom. That is Christ's role, and his alone. Do not try to take it from him because you are not able to fulfil such a demanding task.

Prayer

Lord,
It is a privilege to be part of your bride.
Forgive us when we allow our language to become functional
and we shy away from intimacy with you.
Forgive us when we treat your betrothal to us lightly.
Forgive us when we are unfaithful.

Forgive us when we neglect you.
Forgive us when we are not ready to receive you.
Forgive us when we take you for granted.
Deepen our love for you.
Strengthen our commitment to you.
Enlarge our capacity to welcome you.
Thank you that despite all of the mistakes we make, you still love us! Thank you that you are still committed to us! Thank you that you have prepared a wedding and you will take us to be with you! Thank you that we can look forward with hope, anticipation, and joy to the moment of our reunion. Thank you that our faith shall be made sight.
May we live as your bride with great faithfulness in this world.
May we point to our Lover and to our Groom with gratitude and pride.
May we smile when we mention your name.
May our hearts burst with love for you.
May our actions and decisions demonstrate our commitment to you.
May we never be embarrassed about you holding our hearts.
May we never be ashamed of you.
You are our Groom and we adore you! We love you! We long for you!
Receive our praise and thanks and worship and adoration.
Amen.

DAY *40*

He Will Judge the Living and the Dead

In the presence of God and of Christ Jesus, who will judge the living and the dead, and in view of his appearing and his kingdom, I give you this charge…

2 Timothy 4:1 (NIV)

"When the Son of Man comes in his glory, and all the angels with him, then he will sit on his glorious throne. Before him will be gathered all the nations, and he will separate people one from another as a shepherd separates the sheep from the goats. And he will place the sheep on his right, but the goats on the left. Then the King will say to those on his right, 'Come, you who are blessed by my Father, inherit the kingdom prepared for you from the foundation of the world. For I was hungry and you gave me food, I was thirsty and you gave me drink, I was a stranger and you welcomed me, I was naked and you clothed me, I was sick and you visited me, I was in prison and you came to me.' Then the righteous will answer him, saying, 'Lord, when did we see you hungry and feed

you, or thirsty and give you drink? And when did we see you a stranger and welcome you, or naked and clothe you? And when did we see you sick or in prison and visit you?' And the King will answer them, 'Truly, I say to you, as you did it to one of the least of these my brothers, you did it to me.'

"Then he will say to those on his left, 'Depart from me, you cursed, into the eternal fire prepared for the devil and his angels. For I was hungry and you gave me no food, I was thirsty and you gave me no drink, I was a stranger and you did not welcome me, naked and you did not clothe me, sick and in prison and you did not visit me.' Then they also will answer, saying, 'Lord, when did we see you hungry or thirsty or a stranger or naked or sick or in prison, and did not minister to you?' Then he will answer them, saying, 'Truly, I say to you, as you did not do it to one of the least of these, you did not do it to me.' And these will go away into eternal punishment, but the righteous into eternal life."

Matthew 25:31–46 (ESV)

The return of Jesus Christ will be a day of great blessing for those who trust in him, and a day of great separation and pain for those who have chosen to reject him.

It is in the light of that return that I am charged, as a minister of the gospel and as a servant of Jesus Christ, to ask you to consider your own position before him. When you see him face to face – and you will surely stand before him one day – will you hear the words, "Well done, good and faithful servant," or will you hear the words, "Depart from me... I never knew you"?

Every person who has ever lived will stand before the judgment seat of Christ one day.

It is my profound prayer that you will be ready for that moment.

He invites you to consider who he is, what he has done for you, and how you respond – now.

Please take a moment to talk to the Jesus about whom you have been reading in these pages. He loves you more than you will ever understand and longs to call you friend. His friendship has utterly transformed my life and the lives of countless others around the world throughout the last 2,000 years. All the words that I could write would not explain to you what he means to me.

Why don't you let him tell you himself how much he loves you?

He is only a prayer away.

Prayer

If you have never before committed your life to Christ, then this prayer might help you. Pray it slowly and intentionally, and if you need to, ask someone else to pray with you:

Lord Jesus Christ,
Who came and lived and died and rose again for me, I come to you just as I am.
Kneeling before you, with all of my questions and all of my failings, I invite you to take control of my life.
I acknowledge my weaknesses, my mistakes, and my failings before you.
Forgive me for my wrongdoing.
Wash away my sin.

Strengthen me in my faith and help me to get to know you better as day follows day.
I never knew you loved me this much.
I do not understand everything about you. I probably never will, but I do now want to place my trust in you afresh.
Help me to discover your purpose for my life, and show me what it means for me to be your disciple.
Fill me with your Holy Spirit, guide me through your Word, and enable my path to cross the paths of others who know you, love you, and serve you. Help me to find my place in your body, the church, and let my life count for you.
Thank you for your acceptance of me.
Thank you for what you have done for me.
Thank you for your grace.
Amen.

Prayer

If you are already a Christian, then perhaps this prayer will help you:

Lord Jesus,
Thank you for reminding me of who you are and what you have done for me.
May I never take you for granted.
Help me to grow in my relationship with you.
Continue to reveal yourself to me through the power of your Holy Spirit. Instruct me through your Word. Lead me into greater intimacy and love of your Father.
As I continue to serve you, help me to give you the best of my life.
Thank you for your body, the church.

May I play my part in advancing your kingdom and uplifting your name.
In the moments when I wander, draw me back to your heart.
Do not let me become discouraged by the many ways in which I fail you or the many ways in which your church obscures the beauty of your character and love of your heart.
Instead, let me fall more and more in love with you and become more and more faithful to you.
I surrender to you afresh and look with anticipation to what lies ahead.
Even so, come, Lord Jesus.
Amen.

Thank you

Thank you so much for taking the time to read this little book. I would love to hear from you if it has helped or if you have any questions. Please get in touch with me. It would be wonderful to hear of ways in which the Lord Jesus, the subject of these pages, has touched and transformed your life.

You can stay in touch via the following means:

Twitter: @MalcolmJDuncan
#40DaysWithJesus
Facebook: Malcolm J. Duncan
Facebook Page: 40 Days with Jesus
Email: Office@goldhill.org
Web: www.goldhill.org